# ELECTRIC SOUL

TAYLOR SARACEN

# ELECTRIC SOUL

The Rise Up Series
Book Three
by
Taylor Saracen

13 Red Media Ltd.

PUBLISHER'S NOTE: This is a work of fiction. Names, characters, businesses, places, events, locales, and incidents are either the products of the author's imagination or used in a fictitious manner. Any resemblance to actual persons, living or dead, or actual events is purely coincidental.

ELECTRIC SOUL

Copyright © 2019 Taylor Saracen

All rights reserved. No part of this publication may be reproduced, distributed, or transmitted in any form or by any means, including photocopying, recording, or other electronic or mechanical methods, without the prior written permission of the publisher, except in the case of brief quotations embodied in critical reviews and certain other noncommercial uses permitted by copyright law. The scanning, uploading, and distribution of this book via the Internet or by any other means without the permission of 13 Red Media Ltd. is illegal and punishable by law.

Photography by Alejandro Palomares

Cover Design by Emily Irwin

*To Joey*
*I've never met anybody like you. May your soul continue to be electric and your life more beautiful than even you could imagine. You're a force of nature, and goddamn is your nature good.*

# ACKNOWLEDGMENTS

First and foremost, a big thank you to Keith Miller for understanding and enhancing the vision of this series. I'm perpetually impressed by his foresight and acuity. A special thank you to Cameron Parks for his tireless work ethic, patient ear, and sense of humor. It's a pleasure to work with him. An awed thank you to Emily Irwin for her ability to continuously create art that is more beautiful than I could have imagined. Thank you to Jill Savoia for being my go-to in all areas of everything, for her honesty, and most importantly, for her editing prowess. To Jenifer Friedman for opening my eyes to a world of possibility. Thank you to Bridget and Paige for their input. It was priceless. Finally, a resounding thank you to my family for their endless love and support in all I do.

**ELECTRIC SOUL**

# 1

Joey Mills was born wild. At least that's what his mother had always said. While other kids held tight to their parents' legs during preschool drop-off, Joey had pranced his ass across the room, shockingly independent for a four-year-old. His unearned autonomy had worn Bridget down long before her due. She was a young mother, having had Joey's older sister, Paige, at sixteen and Joey two years later. Though being a teen mom was tough, Bridget hadn't been shy in sharing with Joey that he made it tougher. It wasn't as if she had to say it explicitly, it was something he'd implicitly known. He'd never processed interactions the same way his friends did. He never gave enough of a shit to concern himself with other people's impressions, but maybe that was because he was consistently leaving them impressed.

His childhood had been full of adults fawning over him, taken by his smart mouth and sassy demeanor—attributes that were never an issue before straight-laced teachers made them into negatives rather than the positives they'd always been. It was a strange transition to be revolting after being revered for so long.

"Do you ever feel old?" Joey asked as he leaned down to light the cigarette hanging out of his mouth on the small flame of the single-burner stovetop situated in the "kitchen" of the abandoned trailer that he, Mattie, and Emily had found refuge in.

"Old?" Emily questioned, screwing down her dark brown brows. "Fuck no."

"Fuck no?" Joey laughed, taking a drag as he tossed his lanky body down on the battered booth beside the source of the fire. "Things have been easy for you then?"

"Maybe she's just not as dramatic as you," Mattie teased, sitting on the edge of the ripped leather seat as Joey eyed her incredulously.

"Dramatic?" he repeated, shaking his head as he blew rings of smoke out between his lips. "Tell me something I don't know."

"I thought you were going to dispute it," Emily grinned. "Can you …" she paused, her brown eyes lighting up at his lack of response, "dispute it?"

"I can't do anything I don't feel like doing," Joey admitted, licking his autumn-chapped lips. "It's like I'm not physically capable."

"You're physically capable of more than I imagine any other burnout could be," Mattie noted, tucking the crown of her head into the armpit of Joey's hoodie.

"I mean, I'm not about to run a fucking marathon," Joey replied, pulling his friend further into the snuggle. "Why do people even do that?"

"Run marathons?" Emily asked skeptically. "Specifically? Besides the obvious health benefits?"

"Health, shmealth," Joey tsked. "The only benefit to running a marathon is bragging rights, and honestly, as soon as you mention the miles, nobody cares enough to listen to anything else you say. Five, ten, fifteen," he paused as if he was taking the distance into consideration, "nobody cares."

"If you did it, you would," Mattie stated. "Deny that."

"Like I can," Joey chuckled, watching as his exhale twisted and stretched through the air, long helixes spiraling toward the ceiling. "I literally brag when I get up for school in the morning."

"Which happens, like, once a year," Emily ribbed.

"So exactly how often Michael wants to fuck you," Joey shot back, his smirk mirroring his best friend's.

"Savage prick," Emily chided, unable to hide her amusement. "How do you do that?" she asked, leaning her back against the laminate counter to regard him curiously. "You drag me and I smile."

"People like when someone says what everyone's actually thinking," Joey reasoned, shifting as Mattie attempted to get comfortable in his arms. "What's your problem?"

"I have to poop," she admitted, sitting up abruptly. "Do you think they have toilet paper in the bathroom?"

Joey glanced around the disheveled space and thought it was surprisingly well-stocked for a trailer that had no doubt been deserted by meth heads. "Maybe." He gestured toward a pile of newspapers sitting on the small folding table a few feet away. "Bring a few pages just in case."

Emily chuckled, taking Mattie's spot next to Joey as Mattie retrieved the paper.

"To the grave," Mattie said, pointing her finger at them in warning. "I'm serious. Don't use this as an excuse to tell one of your rambling stories."

"You love my stories," Joey asserted.

"Yeah, when they don't center around me," Mattie conceded. "Whatever. Pretend I'm not about to do what I'm going to do."

"You're making this into a way bigger deal than it needs to be," Emily admonished, waving their friend away. "Just go."

Mattie narrowed her eyes for a moment, one last look of caution before plodding into the bathroom.

"It's cold," Emily stated, manually manipulating Joey's arms around her body.

"It could be colder," he replied sleepily. The Congress vodka they'd taken shots of was finally clouding his head enough to coax his eyelids closed. "It's usually colder by this time of year."

They were in the belly of Fall, a formidable beast in the Midwest. The irony that the town he grew up in was called Pacific and would never live up to its name, while Missouri always would, wasn't lost on

Joey. Oceans were worlds away from the landlocked state—a fortress of crimson sweetgum trees in the country and a cesspool of crime in St. Louis.

"So we're lucky?" Emily offered, earning a chuckle from Joey.

"So lucky," he confirmed, yawning and tugging her in closer. "I don't hate it here."

"In the trailer or Pacific?"

"Either," he replied. He pried one of his eyes open for long enough to notice that the flame below the range had begun to taper. "We're out of gas. We won't be able to light anything if that burns out."

Pulling herself out of his arms, Emily scoured the trash riddled floor.

"What're you doing?" Joey asked, perplexed that his best friend was on her hands and knees on the filthy surface.

"I'm looking for something flammable."

"Oh, that's a great idea," he deadpanned, pulling the bowl of weed that was jabbing him in the thigh out of his pocket. He rolled it in his palms as he watched what had been flares of fire dwindle down to pale blue buds. "We've had worse though."

"No doubt," Emily agreed, holding up an aerosol can of expanding foam. "This should do the trick."

"Watch your eyebrows," Joey cautioned as Emily stood over the stovetop, can in hand.

"That's what you're worried about?" she giggled. "Seriously?"

"Yeah. If you burn them off, they won't grow back. Have you seen people without eyebrows? They look like aliens. You could ruin your whole life right now."

Emily sighed and tapped the side of the can impatiently. "Should I not do it?"

"I never said that. I just said be careful of your eyebrows," Joey reiterated. "Stand back a little more. Give it some distance."

Emily did as she was told as Joey wondered why people were so driven to listen to him in circumstances where he wouldn't have even listened to himself. Still, he didn't mind the power.

He watched as Emily tentatively sprayed the foam at the flame. The reaction was immediate, a bright flash of fire blasting toward the low ceiling as plumes of black smoke billowed from the blaze.

Joey's lungs contracted to tight, tense balls as he coughed wickedly at the pollutant permeating every ounce of air in the trailer.

"We gotta get out of here," Emily uttered between her hacking.

They stumbled to the bathroom door and banged on it frantically to get Mattie moving.

"I'm mid-shit," she yelled. "Go away!"

"Fire," Emily cried, continuing to knock.

"You two are idiots," Mattie growled. The sound of crumpling paper nearly drowning out the sound of fists pummeling plywood.

"Bitch, hurry up," Joey demanded. "You're gonna die in the shitter of a meth den."

Mattie swung the door open and looked to her right. "Really? This is why we can't have nice things." She puffer-fished her cheeks out and Joey did the same, holding his breath as they exited the structure.

They stood a few feet back and observed as the trailer rapidly became engulfed in flames. Long licks of yellow danced across the steel roof, illuminating the blanket of darkness that had descended upon them hours prior.

"This was dumb, even for you," Mattie muttered, shaking her head at Joey. "How'd you do it?"

"I didn't. Emily sprayed some expandable foam shit on the fire to build it up and …" he held his hands up in front of him to present the inferno, "ta-da."

"You didn't tell me not to," Emily reminded.

"I don't tell people not to do things," Joey stated plainly. "If you tell them not to, they usually do it anyway, and if you don't, extraordinary things can happen."

"And this is extraordinary?" Mattie scoffed, blue eyes wide as she gaped at Joey.

He shrugged. "Well, it's not ordinary."

Obviously giving up on reasoning with Joey, Mattie turned to Emily. "You're going to him for advice now?"

Joey clicked his tongue. He should've been insulted by the insinuation, but he wasn't. He wasn't exactly a pillar of good reason. "You can't say it wasn't effective though," he noted. "It did the job."

"The place is on fire," Mattie said as if Joey couldn't see what was right in front of his eyes.

"And what about it?" Joey replied, pushing his hair off his forehead as the trailer incinerated rapidly.

"We should probably go," Emily suggested, concern evident in her voice.

"There's nothing around for miles," Joey said calmly. "It's kinda beautiful, right? I mean, it's destruction, but it's gorgeous in a way too."

"Like you," Mattie asserted, poking Joey in the rib. "And you can't afford to get in any more trouble."

Joey chuckled. He'd been in a near-constant state of "trouble" since fourth grade. Tiptoeing toward destruction was the norm, so much so that when the opportunity to get into more mayhem presented itself to Joey, he was unafraid to walk with his head held high directly into the heat. He knew he should have been more cautious, but he wasn't sure he was built that way. There was no fear of consequence; there was only the moment.

"If it jumps to the trees, we'll legit have caused a forest fire," Emily added. "That has to be arson charges or something." She wrapped her fingers around Joey's wrist and tugged him away from the blaze.

Reluctantly, he followed his friends on the trail they'd taken to get to the mobile home, but not before glancing over his shoulder to get one last look at the mess they left behind—the radiant wreckage of just one night. It was extraordinary.

## 2

A lingering cough and clothes that reeked of smoke were all Joey had to show for the strange events of the night before. He was glad he'd escaped without burns, those would have been a bitch to deal with and difficult to explain to his mother. It was miraculous that Bridget still gave a shit about what Joey did. He couldn't imagine the mental energy it took to worry about someone who didn't worry at all. Every poor decision he made affected him in some way, yet the ramifications were never as powerful as the regret he would feel for missing out on an experience. He couldn't imagine having one life to live and living it contained by the lines society wanted to paint people into.

Rolling out of bed, Joey dragged his tired bones to the shower. Maybe he'd go to school. The trailer fire story would kill in the cafeteria. Sliding his hands up the slick, cool tiles surrounding the shower stall, Joey allowed the steaming water to pummel his sore muscles. For a person who didn't work out, he was constantly achy. It was probably his body's way of telling him he was an asshole for treating it like shit. The fact that he felt geriatric at fifteen didn't bode well for the shape he'd be in if he ever made it to fifty.

Joey sighed as he leaned down to pick up a bar of soap from the ledge of the tub. His classmates' impending appreciation of his recounting of the trailer debacle probably wasn't worth the effort it took to go to school. He hadn't shown up in a few days, and Monday morning meant counseling with Mr. Seaver. Counseling. What bullshit. The only saving grace was that "counseling" was a school board–approved cover for mandatory drug testing. There was no doubt in Joey's mind that the old asses who made the rules thought their idea to offer "counseling" to kids with drug infractions was progressive. It was a joke, but it could have been worse. Seaver could have actually expected Joey to share shit with him. Luckily, all the guy wanted was his piss. He had to start downing his drinks if he was going to give a passable sample.

He never thought his life would be so impacted by pee, but getting caught with melatonin in his bag Freshman year had put urine at the forefront of his mind for way too much of the time. As if being suspended for a sleeping aid wasn't dumb enough, Pacific High School had found a way to make it even stupider by making it a *thing*. At least the surveillance had given Joey the opportunity to hone his ability to test clean despite smoking enough weed to ensure his samples would be indefinitely dirty.

Climbing out of the shower, Joey dried his body, brushed his teeth, and wrapped a towel around his waist before going down to the kitchen so the chugging could commence. As usual, the first five glasses of water went down easily and the following eleven were torture.

"You must be really thirsty," Bridget stated as she entered the kitchen an hour into Joey's process.

"Parched," Joey smirked, well aware that his mother knew what he was doing.

"How many times have I told you that I don't want you smoking weed?"

"As many times as I've ignored you telling me that you don't want me smoking weed," he replied, taking a deep breath and beginning to gulp the water again.

He watched his older sister, Paige, enter the room out of the corner of his eye and smiled around the brim of the glass when she clicked her tongue in true mulish Mills fashion. Joey knew when Paige was poised to go in on their mother, and he was ready to enjoy the show.

"You told him you don't want it in the house," Paige noted, pushing past Joey to pour herself a glass of orange juice. "So technically, he's following your rules—which, I might add, are completely useless."

"They're useless because they're ignored," Bridget said, glaring at her daughter. "Whose side are you on?"

"Mine," Joey answered for his sister. "And it doesn't matter why something's useless if it's useless. It just is."

"You're a real philosopher this morning," Paige laughed, pausing to glare back at Bridget.

"What?"

"Traitor," Bridget tsked, gingerly tugging Paige's long blonde ponytail.

"I've been called worse," she grinned, handing her mother a glass of juice.

"A juice truce," Bridget noted. "Weak."

Joey ignored the exchange, more focused on Paige's philosopher poke. "You know, you should consider purifying your body. Ever since I've been on this cleanse"—he held up his glass for effect—"everything is so much clearer."

"That's the weed still in your system," Paige laughed. "Looks like you've got a lot more drinking to do."

"Don't fuck with my cleanse, Paige," Joey joked, swilling more water down his throat.

"Earlier this week, you were giving her fashion advice for her senior pictures, and now you're pushing cleanses," Bridget grinned. "Are you sure you're not gay?"

"Ha, ha," Joey mumbled sarcastically.

He was. He was sure he was. He had been for as long as he could remember, but he wasn't about to tell her that. Nobody knew. He'd never found it necessary to divulge it because it didn't matter. There were no boys at his school who he was interested in, and even if there were, Joey was pretty positive he was more into weed and trailer fires than he would be into them.

"Anyway, it's all fun and games until somebody else gets too far into it all. I told you before, and I'll tell you again—" Bridget began, only to be cut off by Paige.

"And again, and again, and again."

"I'll keep saying it until it goes through your thick skulls," Bridget scoffed. "Marijuana is the gateway drug. It's the starting line. When you get to heroin and meth, that's the finish. You don't want to be like your father."

"This is literally why I get high," Joey said, refilling his cup. "You talk too much about shit you shouldn't talk so much about."

"I talk so much because you avoid listening to the things you should listen to," Bridget retorted.

"It's just weed, Mom," Paige sighed, looping her arms around the back of Joey's waist to give him a hug. "You're so high-strung sometimes."

"She should smoke more weed," Joey teased, grinning over his shoulder at his sister.

"No doubt," Paige agreed.

"Your dad said it was 'just weed,' too. Then it was pills, coke, heroin, meth," Bridget rattled off, "and look where he ended up."

Dead. He ended up dead, but Joey knew his mother wouldn't say it. She never did. She always alluded to it as though it would be too painful for them if she actually said the word. It wasn't. At least not like Joey thought it should be. What really hurt was his bladder. It was way too full to be ignored.

"Piss number one calls," he said, jogging up the stairs to the sound of his mother telling Paige that she knew mentioning their father 'struck a chord' with him. It was hardly the case, but he wasn't going to argue with his mother over the little bit of power she believed she had over him.

"You're going to be late to school if you don't leave in, like, five minutes," Paige called as she knocked on the door.

"I'm not worried."

"Well, I know you go so infrequently and I figured you'd need to be reminded of how long it takes to actually get there."

"Still not worried," Joey assured her. "I still have eight glasses to go and a liter of Pepsi."

"What's the point of going if you're just going to be tardy and get a detention?"

Joey chuckled, wondering how much longer he was going to have to stand in front of the toilet.

"They don't give me detentions for dumb shit like that anymore. They know there's literally no point."

"Basically you get participation awards for even showing up," Paige decided. Joey could hear the amusement in her voice.

"Exactly."

"You're an interesting one."

"So I've been told."

"Why the Pepsi?" Paige questioned. "To stay awake through your classes?"

"No. After all the water, I have to drink something that makes my pee look darker. If not, they'll know I was diluting my sample," he explained flushing the toilet.

Joey opened the door to see Paige staring at him, flabbergasted.

"Seriously?" She uttered. "Wouldn't it be easier to just not smoke?"

He shrugged. "Maybe, but what would be the fun in that?"

Taking the stairs by twos, Joey went back to his post in the kitchen, continuing the battle with his renal system.

"Do you know what I worry about more than the weed?" Bridget mused as she dunked a piece of toast in a sunny-side-up egg.

"I bet you're going to tell me."

"I will," she nodded. "It's how goddamn stubborn you are."

"It's your fault you had me in May. You made me a Taurus," Joey replied nonchalantly.

"I'm a Taurus and I'm not anywhere near as stubborn as you," Bridget disagreed.

"If I told you that you were, you would stubbornly deny it," Joey smirked, laughing when he saw how unimpressed his mother was at his reasoning. "Anyway ..." he widened his eyes and took a swig of his water.

"Don't forget you work this afternoon."

"When have I ever missed?"

"I could list the times," Bridget offered.

Joey waved his hand, aware of where the conversation was headed. "No, no, no. You're not going to do that. You can't use times when I absolutely could not go because I was otherwise detained against me."

"If you had normal bosses, they would."

"Well, it's good that I don't then," he said simply. "I have to focus or I'm never going to get this done."

"I'm oddly proud that you're at least driven to achieve something," Bridget admitted.

Joey smiled at his mother. "Small victories, Mom."

"Small victories," she sighed. "I'll take them."

"And I'll give them to you."

Sometimes.

## 3

Joey was raised among the wooden booths of D'Antonio's. The pizza joint was as much a home to him as the tract house he grew up in. He was barely two when Bridget began waiting tables at the neighborhood restaurant. With a husband who was more interested in drugs than his family and two small children, she didn't have much of a choice but to get a job that would support them all, at least partially. Jack Mills spent the majority of his wife's earnings on his habit, but that hadn't stopped Bridget from trying to make her kids' lives more comfortable.

Joey wished he had appreciated his mother and her sacrifices more at the time. He wished he could appreciate it more entirely, but it was easy to see past the great things his mother did when she was annoying the shit out of him, and she did that a lot.

"Pick up table four," Bridget directed as she slid behind Joey, who was hunched over the pass with his forehead on the cool metal surface.

Not being hungover was beginning to make Joey feel, well, hungover. It was as if his body functioned better when it was somehow inebriated by a substance most would consider to be a hindrance rather than a help. It was probably an issue, but he wasn't particularly fazed; there were other things to worry about—like why his mother was flicking his ear.

"I'm serious," she asserted. "You better get to them. They already look aggravated."

"Which is probably why you gave them to me to begin with," Joey sighed, standing up to stretch his arms over his head. He grinned down at his mother, who was regarding him unamusedly. "What?"

"Either you're getting taller, or I'm shrinking," Bridget said, studying Joey as if she'd never seen him before that moment. "I think you're getting taller."

"There's probably a better chance of that. I don't think thirty-three-year-olds shrink."

"You've added at least ten years every time you've gotten suspended."

"That makes you like …"—Joey paused to use his fingers to calculate the math in the air in front of him—"nine hundred and ninety years old." He grinned. "You look great."

"Oh, thanks. I'm so glad I look wonderful for a thousand."

"You should start telling people you're a thousand years old. Seriously, they'll be impressed by your preservation."

"You know what would impress me?" Bridget asked, adjusting the tie on her apron.

"Hm?" Joey asked, attempting to check his hair in the side of a large silver mixing bowl. He needed to get it cut. As much as he liked the way it looked when it got a little longer, he couldn't deal with the effort it took to tame the waves.

"If you picked up table four," Bridget stated.

"On my way," he replied without so much as a twitch to indicate he actually was.

In his peripheral vision, Joey saw her roll her eyes, but he decided not to remind her that she had given him her vanity. Instead, he reminded Ernesto that he owed him a cigarette. "Ernie, after I take their order, I want the two I gave you last night."

Ernesto smirked as he expertly tossed a caesar salad and plated it within a five-second span. "Smoked 'em."

"Ah, you're a funny one tonight, huh, troll?" Joey teased, grunting when his mother smacked him upside his head. "What the fuck, Bridge?"

"Troll?" Bridget chided.

"What?" Joey questioned, grinning at Ernesto, who shook his head and laughed in response.

"He likes it. He thinks it's funny. Don't you, Ernie?"

"Forget that I owe you two and I'll lie for you," Ernesto offered, pushing a pie into the pizza oven.

Amused by the statement, Joey chuckled and did a half-spin to meet his mother's unimpressed face. "What?"

"Table four."

"Right," he nodded, checking to make sure his pad was in his pouch. It was, but as usual, he was missing a pen. As he dug around in the deep pocket, he heard his mother sigh with obvious aggravation.

"I'll handle them while you …"—she flapped her arms in front of her as if presenting what a mess Joey was—"figure out how you can be less of a liability."

"Ooh, what a burn!" Caleb complimented, patting Bridget on the shoulder as she made her way back to the dining room. "That one left a mark, didn't it, Joey?"

Perplexed by what the hell his boss was getting at, Joey nodded politely. Though he'd known Caleb and Krista since he was a toddler, Joey was aware that they were the owners first and his surrogate family second.

"The burn," Caleb clarified, companionably clapping Joey on the back. "Your Mom went in hard."

"Oh yeah. She's a savage," Joey replied, crossing the kitchen to grab a pen from the junk drawer beneath the to-go phone. "Where's Krista?"

"That's a great question," Caleb sighed, gesturing to the kitchen as if Joey hadn't already noticed she wasn't in it. It didn't take a detective to recognize that the couple was having issues. "Anything I can help you with?"

"Maybe. A friend of mine wants to apply to serve."

"Oh yeah?"

"Mm-hmm. She's smart, does really good in school and everything."

"Well," Caleb corrected. "She does really well."

"Sure," Joey said easily. "She knows when to use 'well' and 'good' perfectly too, so there's that."

"We appreciate that," Caleb stated, smiling at Joey as Ernesto laughed.

Joey glared at the cook, who narrowed his eyes right back at him. "I'm gonna ignore your giggling."

"Like you ignored table four?" Ernesto asked, appearing to be quite pleased with his comeback.

"This clever motherfucker," Joey chuckled, reaching his hand through the pass to give Ernie some credit where credit was due.

"You like it, huh?" Ernie grinned.

"Not as much as I'm going to like the two you owe me."

"We're back to this now?"

Joey nodded. "Full circle, man. Full circle."

"Tell her to come in tomorrow afternoon, and we'll have a little sit-down," Caleb offered, squeezing Joey's cheek just the way he did when Joey was a kid.

"Thanks," Joey replied, glancing at Ernie, who looked like the cat that ate the canary. Though he appeared to be eager to say something, the cook remained silent until Caleb exited the kitchen.

"That face helps you get away with a lot, doesn't it?" Ernesto asked, shaking his head with mock disapproval, "Those innocent eyes!"

"I literally don't get away with anything."

"Then Bridget must be tired," Sal, a line cook, stated, rolling a cutter through the bubbling cheese of a fresh-from-the-oven pizza.

"She is," Bridget confirmed as she walked into the kitchen. "I'll put in the order, but you're running it."

She stood at the POS, tapping the screen while simultaneously scowling at Joey.

"Fine," he answered, waving her off as if she were a fly persistently buzzing in his ear. "Mattie's gonna work here."

"Do Krista and Caleb know that?" Bridget asked.

"I told Caleb and he said she should come in to talk to him tomorrow."

"You *told* him," Bridget iterated, raising an eyebrow at the wording. "You're the boss now?"

"Always?" Joey offered, immediately dodging the wad of dough that Ernie chucked toward his head.

"He's yours," Sal reminded Bridget.

"As if I could forget," she snarked.

"As if she'd want to," Joey shot back at Sal before wrapping his arms around Bridget's shoulders. "It's cool about Mattie, right?"

"Are you trying to get your whole crew working here?" his mother questioned, ruffling Joey's hair.

"It makes the time pass quicker when you're around people you like."

"Which is why we've been trying to get rid of you for so long," Ernesto teased, chuckling when Joey gave him the finger.

Manually folding Joey's digit down, Bridget informed him, "When that food hits the pass, you better get it out."

"I'm on it," Joey promised.

And he was, balancing plates on a tray as soon as they were ready to go out to the guests.

As usual, he was greeted by the full Midwestern smiles of an elderly couple who were too kind to him right off the bat, with their God-blessed attitudes and early bird eagerness.

"Oh, that looks delicious," the lady crooned, shimmying her crotchety body excitedly. "Have you ever seen a nicer meatball sub, Irv? So saucy!"

"Mmm," her husband nodded, smoothing a napkin over his lap.

Joey wondered how often they spoke, like really talked about things deeper than the aesthetics of a sandwich. They were nearing eighty, if they weren't already there, and had no doubt been together for a large chunk of those years. When did people run out of things to say to one another? There had to be days or years when they had nothing to say. How did they push past those times to be sitting in a booth at D'Antonio's a century later, commenting on balls of beef? Marriage was a fucking mess of commitment. And boring, it was surely boring. It rarely ever worked, and when it did, Joey doubted it was worth the effort.

"You're adorable," the woman commented, smiling at Joey as she shook a jar of parmesan over her sub. "Absolutely precious."

"Thank you," Joey said genuinely. He crossed his arms over his chest and rocked from the balls of his feet to the heels. "Can I get you anything else?"

"We're just great," the man assured. It was obvious from his demeanor that he was waiting for Joey to leave the table to begin his meal.

Conscious of the fact, Joey attempted to turn back to the kitchen, but he was stopped by the cheery woman's cold, shaky hand reaching for his leg.

"I'd like to tell my granddaughter about you. She's at Washington University and a real knockout," she pitched. "She'd find you as handsome as I do. I know it."

"He's fourteen years old," her husband chided, shaking his head in aggravation. "Really, Dee, you can't tell that he's a child?"

"I'm fifteen," Joey corrected, but the point was valid. He didn't feel like a kid, but he was okay with being one if it got him out of a grandparent set-up.

"When you get to be a certain age, everyone looks young," Dee noted. She sighed and lifted half of her sub to her face. "It was worth a try."

"For sure," Joey agreed cordially. He asked them if they needed anything else before hurrying away from the table.

As he walked back to the kitchen, Joey heard Irv giving Dee an earful about how she should "listen to him" and "spend some time on the planet Earth" with him.

While the concept of matrimony was foreign to him, fighting wasn't. That he understood.

# 4

D'Antonio's wasn't a bustling culinary hub, but it did get crazy busy on weekends and game nights. Though Pacific wasn't far from downtown St. Louis, it felt like it was worlds away. Somehow the podunk town had managed to purport itself as a suburb thanks to its proximity to a progressive city. It was an odd juxtaposition for Joey to be caught in a conservative bubble mere miles away from more liberal thought.

The Mills/Reegan family didn't hold the same archaic values most of Pacific's population did, which promised Joey that they would be accepting of his sexuality if they ever found out. Still, he never felt compelled to tell them. It was rare for any emotion or attribute to be monumental to him, but for some reason, the fact that he was gay did feel like a big deal. And though he never spent a significant amount of time trying to figure out why, it was puzzling when Joey did reflect on his motivation to keep his preference private. There was no rhyme or reason, yet he was committed to keeping clandestine.

It wasn't as though Joey hadn't come to terms with his sexuality years earlier. He'd known he was into boys since the third grade. Something about Ryan Thatcher had drawn Joey in, and the butterflies that fluttered in his stomach every time he was around Ryan had been a very apparent indication to Joey that he had a crush on his friend. While the attraction wasn't sexual at the time, there was no denying that Joey had craved time with the other boy.

The fact that Ryan had been a consistent claimant of the coveted backseat of the bus—a position of power in elementary school politics—had prompted Joey to wonder if his interest in Ryan were simply a twisted bit of jealousy. When he began sitting with the other kid every afternoon, Joey realized his feelings weren't anything but total adoration. The more Joey liked Ryan, the less time he had spent with him. It may have been a conscious decision, but back then it didn't feel that way. There was nowhere any of it could have gone, so Joey had let it go when he found himself getting annoyed at Ryan for the attention he showed to other friends.

Ryan illuminated two—somewhat obvious—truths for Joey. One, he was gay. Two, there was no benefit in caring too much about any one person. Devotion was the fast track to disappointment, and even at the age of eight, he had been let down by those he cared for too many times to be anything other than tentative. It was par for the course for a kid who was unlucky enough to have a junkie father. Bridget had done her best to shield Joey from the special brand of difficulties, but there was really no saving someone from a person who had such an insatiable need for drugs.

Joey never allowed his mind to wander to thoughts of his father often enough to be affected by the disappointment. It was strange to perseverate on him anyway. Jack had tossed his life away before the accident and again after. He shouldn't have lived. He knew it, everyone knew it, but he had. Joey always wondered why. Why Jack was given another chance just to piss it away. Why kids died of cancer while his father was granted what he had not deserved. Joey blamed the universe for the inequity, but he blamed his father more for not taking advantage of it. He should've died in that truck, but when he didn't, he should've committed himself to living.

In a bizarre way, Joey understood how easy it was to take your life for granted. He didn't worry about death, mostly because he could never imagine himself dead and also because he was pretty sure when he died he wouldn't know he was dead. His soul would dissipate into the thin air that floated around his lifeless body, and he wouldn't be anything anymore. There was no use being pressed about nothing, even when nothing was exactly what he would become.

Paige's views were different. She missed her father in the way a child should. She didn't mourn what he represented or the position he was supposed to hold, she cried for him—the man, not the post. It was confusing how two people who were raised in the same environment, born in close succession, could see it all so disparately. Despite the fact that Joey and Paige argued about stupid shit like siblings do, they were typically on the same page about the important things. Jack was the exception. When it came to his father, emotions that Joey struggled to understand were easily accessed by Paige. She'd never built the walls that Joey had years before, and he honestly didn't know who was worse off. Was it Paige with her open wound? Or was it him and how stitched up he'd become? He wasn't sure if he repressed his feelings so much that they didn't exist or if he'd become so cold that he couldn't recognize them. Either way, they weren't there —and that was okay with Joey.

It wasn't as though Joey ever sat around thinking that he needed to have his father in his life. Perhaps it was because Steve had stepped into that role seamlessly, or because Joey didn't do well with authority to begin with. Despite how long Joey's stepdad had been around, Steve had never attempted to be looked at as anything more than Bridget's husband, which in turn made Joey see him in a positive light.

And when it came down to it, there were worse role models to have than Steve Reegan. If Joey had had any corporate, nine-to-five dreams, he would have idolized his stepdad. Steve was a businessman and a hard worker. He'd busted his ass in his twenties, and by the time he'd hit thirty, he ran a construction company that employed over two thousand people, one of which was Jack Mills.

Bridget and Steve's love story was unconventional to say the least. Following his near-fatal accident, Jack spent months in the hospital.

He went from being in a coma to awake but incapacitated. The whole ordeal had been terrifying for Joey. He was only seven at the time and seeing his otherwise strong father so frail and weak taught him more about mortality than he probably had the right to know. Evidently, the accident was illuminating for Bridget in a different way. She'd spent too much time worrying about a man who lived his life so recklessly, and she wasn't willing to do it anymore.

Bridget met Steve at a company Christmas party. Jack was still in the hospital and Bridget went in his place to thank everyone for their generosity in the wake of her husband's accident. Perhaps it was love at first sight or maybe it was her craving for comfort. Either way, Bridget had forged a special relationship with Jack's boss and served Jack with divorce papers as soon as he was properly coherent.

Joey never blamed his mother. She was a fighter, a survivor, someone who had struggled more than her due. The fact that she had done something for herself after years of worrying about everyone else wasn't worthy of ire. Plus, Steve was a catch. He was wealthy, committed, and sober—three attributes Jack had perpetually lacked. After years of living in turmoil, Joey and Paige were in a stable household with their mother, stepfather, and stepsister, Nicole. Things felt normal, bordering on idyllic, which was great for everyone, but boring for Joey. His interest in excitement trumped his need for order. While others were tentative about change, Joey thrived on it. The more things stayed the same, the more he wanted to fuck shit up. There was no intrigue in the status quo, so he found other ways to keep his mind engaged.

"You alive, Mills?" Mattie asked, kicking Joey's ankle as they lay on the old plaid couch in her basement.

"If I was dead, could I do this?" Joey replied, tilting his pelvis up and gyrating his hips into the air in an overtly sexual way.

"What the fuck is that?" Emily chortled from where she was lounging on the floor. "You just went from catatonic to creepy in two seconds."

"That was something I never want to see again," Mattie laughed, shaking her head as Joey continued the movement. "Literally, I'd rather be dead than see that again."

"So dramatic," Joey tsked, pulling himself up only to plop his body down on Mattie's.

She squealed as he kept grinding.

"She likes it," he told Emily, who coughed on the hit she was taking from the three-foot glass bong standing proudly beside her. "She does!"

Mattie giggled as she pushed Joey off. "You'd be a mediocre stripper."

"Wow," Joey grinned, rolling to the ground to take a rip from the bong. "That's probably the nicest thing you've said to me this year."

"Ever," Emily corrected.

"Which makes you a total cunt considering I got you a job at D'Antonio's," Joey noted, blowing a plume of smoke in Mattie's face.

Mattie smiled and wafted it toward her nostrils. "Am I forever in your debt now, dickface?"

Joey shrugged. "Maybe."

"If he had a dickface, you'd be sucking it," Emily remarked, earning a pillow to her face from a mock-aghast Mattie.

"Make all the jokes you want, but I'm the only one getting any," Mattie stated, twirling her long locks.

"How do you know I'm not?" Joey asked, raising an eyebrow.

"Those moves you just debuted confirmed my suspicions," Mattie replied. "No girl is gonna see that and spread her legs for you."

"Truth," Emily agreed. "She'd dry up like this." She snapped for emphasis and shook her head. "No doubt."

"I give"—Joey paused to inhale from the bong, letting the weed constrict his lungs—"not one single fuck."

"Do you give a fuck about anything?" Emily wondered, grabbing the piece from Joey.

"I give a fuck about you smoking your weight in weed right now," Joey answered, taking the bong back. "I'm not high enough."

"You were just over there trapped in your feelings," Mattie

reminded, gesturing at the couch where Joey had been lying moments earlier.

"My what?" he questioned, drawing the smoke up and listening to the familiar sound of bubbling water.

"Feelings."

"Don't know anything about them," Joey smirked. "All I know about is my sick dance moves and this dank shit."

"You wish. We know you cry inside at least four times a week," Emily teased. "All those repressed emotions—" she began.

"Literally don't exist," he interrupted. "Get as good as me and you'll see."

"That didn't make any sense," Mattie said, rolling her eyes.

Joey held out the bong. "Smoke more and it will."

As far as Joey was concerned, the answer to life's hard questions was to think less about them.

## 5

Joey had always thought of himself as an open book. If people asked him how he felt about a topic, he was never tentative to share his opinions—whether they liked them or not. He was as outspoken as he was confident, so differing viewpoints never intimidated him. In fact, the opportunity to get into a heated debate made his blood course more quickly through his veins. There was something invigorating about clapping back on an ignorant or ill-thought-out argument. If he liked school better, he would have considered applying himself so he could get into college and take the steps necessary to become a lawyer. The issue with the pre-law path was that he hated school more than he loved the endorphins he got when he was shooting down someone's pedestrian points.

Joey's distaste for all things scholastic was a relatively recent development. Through fifth grade, he was a straight-A student, committed to bringing exemplary marks home to his mother, who was unabashedly pleased with his commitment. It wasn't until he hit middle school that good grades lost their luster. He valued afternoons fucking around with his friends more than homework. Detention wasn't intimidating to him and neither were big fat Fs on his report card. The only ramification that worried Joey was the possibility of not matriculating with his peers, but as soon as he realized the threats of being held back were empty, he entirely tuned out. School became a prolonged social hour, and that shift made him hate it less. If all that was required of him was to show up, he was down for it.

It turned out there was an expectation that Joey, like other students, would attend school sober—a rule that became more difficult as time passed. His first drug infraction had been an innocent mistake, but taking the melatonin pills to school had put him on the administration's radar. They were over-the-counter and barely inebriating, but for some reason, they were an absolute scandal for his middle school principal. The most ridiculous part of the whole crackdown was the fact that Joey actually used the melatonin the way it was intended. He'd had insomnia for as long as he could remember and needed the aide. Though he couldn't explain how the pills ended up in his bag, Joey thought he'd made a compelling argument of his innocence. The principal didn't agree and issued Joey a long-term suspension—the heaviest punishment in the handbook for a non-narcotic drug violation. Unfortunately, the mishap had made it impossible for Joey to get anything past the watchful eyes of teachers and support staff.

"Ah, Mr. Mills. How goes it?" Mr. Seaver greeted as Joey walked into the counselor's office for his weekly test.

"How am I supposed to respond to that weird shit? Should I say, 'It goes' like some middle-aged dude would?" Joey asked, flopping himself onto the chair across from Seaver's. He'd been in the school for approximately two minutes and he was already bored out of his mind. He wasn't sure if it was the fluorescent lighting or an abounding aura of academics in the air, but something about the building made him lethargic.

"That's my typical response," Mr. Seaver admitted, narrowing his eyes when Joey held out his hands as if his point had been made. "So, how's the test going to turn out this week?"

"The same as it has for the last eight," Joey replied, examining his wrecked nail beds. He really needed to stop biting his nails. It had become painful to press his fingers against anything, especially his rolling papers when he attempted to keep a blunt tight. "I told you I don't fuck around with weed anymore."

"Language," the counselor reminded with a tsk. "How many times do I have to tell you to watch your language?"

"How many times do you think you have?" Joey wondered. It had to have been at least thirty. "Fuck" had become a pause word for him, much to the chagrin of every single one of his teachers. There was enough to discipline him for that they seemed reluctant to add something as trivial as profanity to the list.

"Enough," Mr. Seaver decided, leaning over to open the bottom drawer of his desk. He slid a collection cup to Joey and sighed. "Let's get it going so you can get to second period."

"I'm in no rush."

"Yeah, I'm aware. Do you think you'll ever make it here in time to get to P.E.?"

"I'm not sporty," Joey said, rolling the cup between his palms.

"Maybe you would be if you showed up to gym class," Mr. Seaver offered.

"Doubtful. And you know what I'm okay with?"

Mr. Seaver shrugged and waited for Joey's response.

"That," Joey replied. "I'm okay with *that*."

"Well good."

Joey stood up, slung his bag over his shoulder, and began to walk toward the staff restroom.

"Backpack!" Mr. Seaver called after him.

Rolling his eyes, Joey turned around and tossed his backpack into Seaver's office. "You really think I'm hoarding bottles of piss in my bag?"

"I think you're a clever kid," the counselor shrugged. "And I can't be too cautious."

"I should be insulted."

"Are you?"

Joey shook his head, "Nope."

"What does it take to insult you, Mills?" Mr. Seaver wondered with a smirk.

"More than you could ever dish out," Joey assured.

He made his way to the restroom, tore the seal, and filled the cup. Taking the time to examine its contents, Joey hummed his approval. Damn, he was consistent. As he washed his hands, he considered his need for a new hobby. He shouldn't have spent so much time concerned about piss. The most exciting part of his day would no doubt be when his test came back clean, confirmation that he tricked the system yet again. There had to be more interesting things to do with himself. Everything was so stagnant and he was compelled to be anything but.

Joey placed the sample on the small unit in the corner of the bathroom, switched places with Seaver, and awaited the verdict.

"You're good to go," Mr. Seaver reported, putting the remaining testing strips back into his desk.

Joey gave the counselor a cheeky grin. "As expected."

"Well, by you. I don't care how many times you pass them, Joseph. I always think you're going to come up dirty," Mr. Seaver.

"First off, my name isn't Joseph. It's Joey. Like, Bridget named me Joey. I'm just Joey. Period. Second, aren't you supposed to be empowering me and shit? You're literally telling me you don't think I've stopped smoking weed even though it's *illegal* and I've been in trouble, like, five hundred and forty-two times."

"That's precisely the issue, 'Just Joey.' You've been in trouble five hundred and forty-two times and you didn't stop. It would be naive of me not to be skeptical of your new leaf. I'm here to keep you on track and that means acknowledging your shortfalls and combatting them before they lead to bigger issues."

"While you're doing that, I'm going to go to class."

It was a sad state of affairs when Joey would rather go to math class than waste time with Seaver. Despite the fact that he held an annoying post, the counselor wasn't bad company. Joey imagined that he was probably a lot of fun to be around when he was younger. Though his appearance was clean cut, he hadn't completely lost the hippie vibe that, thanks to an array of peace and equality stickers, was still present on the back bumper of his fifteen-year-old Volvo.

Joey should have been a teenager in the 1960s. All that peace, love, and weed—it was more his speed than being a child of the millennium. People back then had banded together for worthy causes. They were a part of a more artistic culture, where talent was exalted more than media. Maybe he needed to tap into that spirit rather than exist so soullessly. It was too easy to be complacent when nothing was moving around him. He wished his life were charged by a rush of power, volts of energy that made even the most mundane moments electric. He had always been a live wire, and he wanted the world around him to be as lit as he was.

He needed to get outside more. It had been a couple of weeks since the trailer fire, and he was yearning to get in touch with his own nature. Running down dark trails with his friends, twigs snapping under sneakers as they headed toward nowhere in particular, looking for the next adventure. He needed to do something to feel alive because school was killing him.

Pulling his phone out of his pocket as he meandered to math class, Joey shot off a message to his group text.

*Joey (9:17am): Tonight*

*Emily (9:18am): Tonight what?*

*Joey (9:18am): Let's have fun. We can go to the woods behind the Westcotts' abandoned farmhouse and look for Native American daggers and shit.*

*Mattie (9:19am): As fun as it sounds to look for objects that aren't there in the pitch darkness, I have a shift tonight.*

*Joey (9:19am): Blow it off.*

*Mattie (9:19am): I've been working there for 2.2 minutes and you vouched for me. Wouldn't that make you look bad?*

*Joey (9:20am): The only thing that makes me look bad is yellow. That shit is horrendous on me.*

He laughed quietly at himself as he walked into the classroom and slid into his seat.

"So nice of you to join us, Joey," Ms. Markel stated as she frantically wrote a formula on the white board. And here he had thought he made it in unnoticed.

"Piss test," he replied matter-of-factly.

His classmates giggled as Ms. Markel glanced over her shoulder to give him an unimpressed glare.

Nonplussed, Joey went back to his messages.

*Mattie (9:20am): Stupid.*

*Joey (9:23am): I agree.*

*Mattie (9:23am): I meant you.*

*Joey (9:23am): Oh, I meant you not going out with Em and me tonight.*

*Emily (9:24am): Who said I was coming?*

*Joey (9:24am): Me.*

*Mattie (9:25am): Tell him no, Emily.*

*Emily (9:25am): You know that's not possible. He'll annoy me until it's a yes. I'd rather just go with it and spare myself.*

*Joey (9:25am): So we're on for tonight, Em?*

*Emily (9:26am): Confirmed.*

*Joey (9:26am): It's going to be dope.*

He couldn't wait.

# 6

Thanks to suburban sprawl, it was necessary for Joey to ride his bike to his friends' houses. It would have been nice if Emily and Mattie lived in his development, but he wasn't that lucky. Instead, he shared a yard line with Elizabeth Chandler, the snobbiest girl in his sophomore class. He figured an attitude like hers would have been backed up by some excessive level of wealth, but she was just a middle-class cunt like him.

Still, Elizabeth was spoiled. It was common knowledge that she had a BMW waiting in the garage for her in anticipation of her sixteenth birthday. Much to Joey's amusement, she offered tours to confirm the rumors and show off the car she'd eventually be parking at the high school. His peers were impressed, and he couldn't say he wasn't. Joey liked the finer things in life. He coveted the clothes, glasses, and designer bags he saw on Instagram influencers. There wasn't much of a chance he'd have the opportunity to afford any of it on his measly D'Antonio's paycheck, but it didn't stop him from dreaming.

While he definitely had some label envy, it wasn't a vapid interest. Joey liked beautiful things, be it an exceptionally hued autumnal leaf or a pair of expertly structured shoes. There was something special about quality, something majestic about perfect pigments and elegant lines. In his wildest dreams, he was a painter or clothing designer, someone who created gorgeous art for a living, someone who could afford to be creative both in trade and craft. Maybe in the future, he could find a way to marry his interest and talent, but until then, he was convinced that pushing the flicker of ambition to the back of his mind was the best course of action. He had better things to do. Like search for arrowheads.

"It's gonna be pretty badass," Joey remarked as he and Emily peddled down the long stretch of road that led to the Westcott farm.

"What is?" she asked, quietly cursing the rock that nearly tossed her off her bike.

"You alright over there?" Joey asked, concerned by her exaggerated movements.

"I'm fine. It's been a while since I rode."

"If Mattie were here, I'd make a really funny joke," Joey informed his friend.

"Saying that means you practically just did," Emily laughed. "We always give her shit, but I think we're the freaks."

"Speak for yourself."

"You're not a freak?"

"Only in the best possible ways," Joey assured her.

"You think searching for Native American relics is 'badass.' That's what you were talking about, right? The arrowheads?"

Joey lifted his eyebrows in mock challenge. "And what of it?"

"Freak," Emily asserted with a wink.

"Says the fucking bookworm."

"There are a lot of things you could say to me that would probably insult me, but calling me a 'bookworm' isn't one of them. That's basically giving me shit for being smarter than you."

"And?"

"And that's really dumb," Emily laughed.

"Who says you're smarter than me anyway?"

"Your grades, our teachers, your face," she teased, yelping when Joey purposely swerved his wheels at hers. "Asshole."

"Drag me on whatever you want, but you know I give good face."

Emily glanced at Joey and chuckled when he puckered his lips like a duck and gave her a sultry stare.

"Look at it," he urged, snickering when she turned her head away. "C'mon."

"Don't make me laugh. I'll fall off."

"So dramatic," he tsked, pumping his legs faster up the hill. "If you fall, you get back on. Isn't that what they always say?"

"I think that's about horses," Emily called from a few yards behind him.

"What's the difference?"

"Life," she replied. "Slow down."

"Speed up," Joey retorted, stopping at the top of the hill to wait for his struggling friend.

The freezing air was laden with the smell of burning wood and winter, though the season's first snow hadn't fallen yet. Gazing up at the dark pinhole sky, Joey took a deep inhale, allowing his lungs to be invigorated by the freshness rather than the dank they were used to. There were nights when the world felt just as magical as it did when he was inebriated when he was sober. The wonders of life hadn't been deadened by the hunger for a high his father had been afflicted with.

Realistically, Joey knew why his mother worried about him. He had fucked up blood and a propensity for addiction. It was as though the monster who resided deep inside him was constantly waiting to engulf him. What Bridget didn't understand was that he was more powerful than any craving he'd ever had. While he didn't look at the illness as a weakness, he considered his ability to remove himself from his wants a strength. Some people didn't have the capacity to put their mind over invading matter. Joey definitely did. He attributed the skill to his stubbornness. The character trait his family considered his greatest flaw was probably the thing that saved his life time and time again.

"This isn't fun," Emily reported as she rolled up to Joey just in time for him to continue toward the abandoned building. "Really?" she yelled, the exasperation evident in her tone.

Joey laughed into the wind, tears beading in the corners of his squall-slapped eyes. He was happy. He felt that. Forty-five minutes of fresh air and freedom had assuaged the anxiety he'd experienced earlier in the day. It was rare for him to be so overtaken by an emotion that wasn't tied to a specific event, but something about the moment was magic. The world was different than it had been minutes before, he was the same, and that was okay because he wasn't expected to be anything more.

Peddling up to the driveway of the old house, he waited for Emily to catch up. Though the cold had caused tear streaks to stain her face, Joey doubted she'd had as cathartic a ride as he did, but he could see in her eyes that the night didn't suck for her as much as she pretended.

They kicked their kickstands and left their bikes on the pavement before trekking into the woods behind the farmhouse. Reaching into his backpack, Joey handed Emily a flashlight and grabbed one for himself. He didn't always come prepared, but when he did, it was because he was really into what he was doing.

"So, are you going to tell me why you dragged me out here to look for arrowheads?"

"Are you going to tell me why you don't think it's the best fucking idea ever?" Joey questioned, draping his arm over Emily's shoulders. "What if we find one? Mike Harrison claims he did last week. I guess he made it into a necklace."

"That seems ..."—Emily paused as if she was searching for her feelings on the statement—"sacrilegious."

"How could it be sacrilegious? He's not Native American, and it has nothing to do with their religion anyway."

"How do you know? Aren't you failing history class?"

"Look at you with the low blows," Joey laughed. "What does that have to do with anything? Getting shitty grades doesn't mean I'm an idiot. It just means I don't give a shit about grades."

"Which is dumb to begin with," Emily stated.

"Like you set the world on fire with your scores? Last I checked, the only thing you've lit up lately was that old trailer," Joey teased.

"That was a group effort," Emily asserted, shaking her head in disapproval. "Ugh, I'm annoyed that you'd even bring that up."

"Why? It was crazy."

"You don't feel guilty?"

"Guilty?" Joey asked, flabbergasted by her use of the word. In his mind, they hadn't done anything wrong. It was the owner's abandonment that created the problem to begin with. He could have probably said the same about his dad. Perhaps he would have been more affected by the destruction if he allowed himself to be impacted by anything at all.

"Guilty," Emily confirmed, shining her flashlight at a particularly dense bush. "I thought that was a dog."

"A dog?" Joey chuckled. "That would be a fat-as-fuck mutt."

"It would be, but I bet he'd be a good cuddle buddy."

Raising an eyebrow, Joey asked, "Is that all it takes to be with you?"

"Who are you asking for?" Emily retorted.

"Certainly not myself."

"Well duh."

Joey was taken aback by the confidence behind her statement. Did she *know*? There was no way she could. There was no way anybody could. He barely allowed himself think about guys. Joey wasn't sure why he felt compelled to be secretive about it, but he did, and it wasn't worth the mental energy it would take to figure it out.

"What do you mean 'duh'?" he asked despite himself.

"You're my best friend. It would be weird to think of you that way," Emily replied matter-of-factly. She narrowed her eyes. "What are you getting at?"

"Nothing," Joey answered quickly. "Absolutely nothing."

"You don't want me to think of you that way, do you?" she asked. Though it was dark, Joey could see the confusion written all over her face.

"No," he scoffed, as if the idea was ludicrous. It was.

"Oh my goodness," Emily began, shining a beam of light on a small clearing cluttered with sticks and rocks. "Is that ...?"

"What?" Joey questioned, quickly focusing his flashlight on the area. "Do you see something?" His heart started to race as he considered the chance that they may actually find what he hoped for.

Emily inched forward. "I see ... absolutely nothing."

"Fuck you!" Joey cried. "You got me super excited."

"Yeah, and you got me out in here in the middle of the night. We're even."

"It's, like, eleven. That's hardly the middle of the night," Joey chuckled.

He bathed the sticks and rocks with light one more time before suggesting that they get out of there.

"Finally," Emily sighed, following closer to Joey as they made their way to their bikes.

She was scared. He could feel it. And he didn't relate to the fear at all.

## 7

The arrowhead excursion ended without a souvenir, but Joey still considered the night a success. It was nice to feel whatever it was he'd felt when he was riding his bike to the farm. Though his body was in Pacific, his mind had gone somewhere else. It usually took weed to achieve a cerebral escape, but somehow joy had facilitated a comparable high. He wondered if the feeling was similar to what religious zealots experienced when they held their hands up toward the heavens and cried in awe at the power of their God. He wondered if he'd tapped into that devotion by appreciating the hulking universe as a whole, if it was a prayer to the ebony sky dotted with diamonds or the corn fields that cast ominous shadows on rocky roads in the silver moonlight. It wasn't often that he considered how insignificant he was, how small he was in relation to the world around him and the world's people didn't know of yet. He wanted to feel that way—wonderstruck by the great beyond, humbled by the possibilities surrounding the soulless population. Feeling pain was better than not feeling at all. The latter was commonplace, and he was different, whether he wanted to be or not.

Joey didn't know what he wanted to be. He wasn't even sure what he didn't. All he knew was that he thought about it less than other people who were trying to mold themselves into certain boxes they were convinced they needed to fit into. He'd always fit in just being himself. Or maybe that was what he'd trained his brain to believe, that he was who he wanted to be, and people wanted to be around whoever he was. Thinking about it too much was a dangerous exercise in self-doubt, one he didn't have the patience to participate in. Why didn't he tell people he was gay? Why was that off-limits if he truly didn't worry about what people thought of him?

For someone who didn't actually have sex, he found his sexuality oddly significant. He knew what he wanted and who he was attracted to, but he'd never acted on the draw. Fuck, it hadn't even been a year since his first kiss with a boy, yet he couldn't define himself completely unless he acknowledged the fact that he was gay. He was a son, a brother, a friend, and he was gay. He was a stoner, a creative, a fuckup, and he was gay. It was the focus of so many of the internal assessments he took of himself, and he was pretty sure that made him a hypocrite. If it was so much of him and he was so unconcerned about people's thoughts on him, why did he feel compelled to hide it? He was just as bad as his classmates, who squeezed into the compartments they built around themselves. Either way, Joey's momentary catharsis on the bike was validation that he felt more trapped than he'd ever admitted to himself. It was a release he hadn't known he needed, and he needed to know why it mattered as much as it did. All he knew was that he didn't want to worry about worrying about something. He didn't want to overthink his emotions just because they were present. They could easily be ignored.

"You're avoiding table nine," Bridget stated as she entered the kitchen.

Joey was leaning on the pass, bullshitting with Ernie and most certainly avoiding table nine.

"False," he replied, not bothering to glance at his mother. He could see her glare, though he didn't lay eyes on her. He'd seen it enough to memorize its attributes.

"True," his mother asserted, slapping his butt with her pad. "C'mon. I'm not picking them up."

"What do you have against high school football players? I thought you were cool with a lot of them when you were in school," Joey teased, earning another whack from Bridget.

"I should've washed your mouth out with soap when I could," she tsked.

"I didn't curse," Joey laughed. "That's for cursing."

"I should have washed your brain with soap," Bridget corrected. She tapped his forehead with mock aggression. "Your *brain*."

"Honestly, you probably should've. There's some wild shit in there."

"I don't doubt that," Ernesto inserted. He pointed at Joey and shook his head at Bridget. "He's wild."

"You don't know the half of it," she promised the cook.

"Yeah, neither do you," Joey replied. "Where's Mattie?"

"She's taking care of her tables," Bridget answered. She pointed at the door to the dining room. "Go."

Realizing he wasn't going to be able to pawn the table off on his friend, Joey straightened his green D'Antonio's t-shirt and headed into the dining room. There were six of them, which should have meant he would get a good tip, but he knew he probably wouldn't. The only kids from his school who tipped well were the ones who waited tables or had parents who did. Football players had practice, they didn't have shifts at pizza parlors.

"Hey. How are you guys doing?" Joey greeted as he approached the table. "What drinks would you like?"

"Beer," Jock One said nonchalantly, tapping his fingers against the menu.

"You don't just order 'beer,'" Jock Two whispered. "You gotta tell him what kind."

"A cold beer," Jock One clarified.

"You're literally wearing your varsity jacket," Joey laughed. He gestured at the rest of the guys. "All of you are."

"They could be old. We could be juniors in college, reliving our glory days," Jock Three offered with a smirk.

"Yeah, that would be super pathetic," Jock Four tsked. "I don't even want to play along with that. Beer isn't worth it."

"I wouldn't have fallen for it anyway," Joey stated. "So, do you want water, Coke, Mountain Dew, something else? We have pitchers."

"We'll get two pitchers of Coke," Jock Four decided quickly. It was apparent from his affect that he was embarrassed by his friends.

Joey nodded. "Got it. Do you need more time with the menu or do you know what you're having?"

"Are we doing the Meat Lover's pies and garlic knots?" Jock Five asked.

"What about wings?" Jock Two questioned. "We have to get something with protein."

Jock Four rolled his eyes. "The pizza has a ton of protein."

"I can come back with your drinks and give you some more time to figure it out," Joey offered as he began to walk away.

"So, you're coming back with my cold beer, then." Jock One uttered with no trace of amusement in his voice.

"Not happening," Joey replied over his shoulder.

It should have been a crime for impressive muscles and chiseled features to be wasted on a guy like that. Not one ounce of the dude's attitude was attractive to Joey, yet somehow he could see past it when he focused on the cuts of his jaw and the bulge of his bicep. He bet the dumb jock would be good in bed.

Joey had never been fucked before, but he was sure he wanted to be. There wasn't much to like about the football player, and in spite of that, Joey couldn't think of anything but being on his hands and knees while the guy plowed him.

Shaking his head as if he'd just swallowed a bitter pill, Joey filled two pitchers with ice and soda.

"What's your problem?" Mattie asked, tickling Joey's side as he sloughed her off. "Cranky," she tsked.

"Not cranky."

"What are you, then?" she pressed, hands on her hips.

Horny. Confused. Sober. Tired. Bored. There were a lot of ways that Joey could have answered the question, but he decided that "annoyed" was the most apropos.

"At those football players?" Mattie wondered, rising to her tippy toes to get a view of the guys. "A few of them are cute, so at least there's that."

Joey clicked his tongue as he wiped the exterior of the pitchers with a paper towel.

"But I guess that doesn't matter much to you," she continued, placing her hand on Joey's shoulder. "Too bad it's not girls from the cheer squad, right? Maybe that would make it suck less."

"What would make it suck less is you taking them," Joey said, earning a chuckle from Mattie. "What?"

"I don't hate myself enough to do that voluntarily. They're going to leave you, like, three bucks if you're lucky."

"What happened to 'a few of them are cute, so at least there's that?'"

"I was just trying to say something that would make *me* feel better about busting my ass for a bunch of douches who would no doubt stiff me," Mattie admitted.

"And that's the best you could come up with?"

Mattie thought for a moment before nodding her head. "Yeah, that's the extent of it."

Unenthused, Joey sighed and walked over to the table. Pouring the cola into each of the guys' red plastic glasses, he listened to them argue over what he assumed was a play.

"It's on Carson," Jock Two asserted. "He's been lagging, and it's completely throwing off the tempo."

"He's fast as fuck," Jock Four disagreed. "Jeff needs to get faster."

"I'm fast as a motherfucker," Jock Six cried, tossing packets of parmesan across the table at his teammate.

Joey sighed, trying to keep it together. "Have you guys figured out what you want?"

"That beer," Jock One stated, lifting his eyebrows and holding his hand out in aggravation.

"Ignore him," Jock Four directed. "We'll have four Meat Lover's pizzas, three dozen wings, and two orders of garlic knots with extra sauce."

"Damn," Joey muttered as he scribbled the order. "For the wings, do you want mild, medium, or hot?"

"One of each," Jock Four said.

Joey nodded. "Got it. Anything else?"

"That beer," Jock One repeated.

The guys at the table groaned and Joey rolled his lips in tight before walking away from the table. It took a lot to get under his skin, but that asshole was buried deep.

For the most part, Joey loved waiting tables. He was outgoing and it was a fun way to make money while bullshitting with people. The problem was sometimes he had to deal with people's bullshit.

"Make the hot wings atomic," Joey told Ernie as he took his usual spot leaning against the pass.

"Those guys are dicks."

"Can't do that," Ernie chuckled.

"They ordered one basket hot, so just make them really hot."

"Joey," Bridget warned from the other end of the kitchen. "Don't be a dumbass."

Mattie laughed. "Sage advice from mama Mills."

"Always," Bridget grinned. "Somebody has to tell him."

"Lucky me," Joey said sarcastically.

But he knew he was.

## 8

For Joey, there were a few good things about having a sister who was two years older than him. The most obvious of which was the fact that Paige had a car and could drive it to parties being thrown in towns too far away for Joey to ride his bike to. Though she always made a big deal about carting his ass around, Joey knew Paige enjoyed his company. They fought like typical siblings, but she was the first person he went to when shit hit the fan and he knew she did the same. They barely broke a sweat when they pulled each other through the hard times. The stamina they'd built was an odd benefit to enduring the boatload of tough stuff that they had. It had made them strong in a way that people who didn't suffer a series of losses could never be. They didn't react to pain in the same way others seemed to. They'd learned how to manage it differently from them, and in some sense, different from each other.

Paige was softer than Joey, which wasn't saying much, but she was. She occasionally felt bad for herself, something he refused to do. He was far more empathetic toward other people's issues than he was sympathetic about his own. His sister insisted that he wasn't dealing with things properly and that one day all the hurt would consume him. He didn't tell her that sometimes it snuck its way into his body and refused to leave until he washed it away with alcohol or burned it up with smoke. He feared that acknowledging it would make it real and he wasn't willing to knowingly do that.

"Pass it," Paige ordered.

Joey glanced up from his hit to see his sister's pale blue eyes regarding him impatiently in the rearview mirror.

"You're hogging it," she stated, reaching her hand back and turning it palm up for the pipe. "C'mon."

Reluctantly, Joey gave her the pipe and leaned back as best he could in the middle seat. Somehow, he always ended up sitting bitch when he was in the back, even though Emily and Mattie had shorter legs than his. He watched his sister take a drag before handing it to her best friend Lilly, who had annoyingly commandeered the passenger seat.

"Do you ever get sick of hanging out with girls?" Lilly wondered, blowing a line of smoke up toward the sunroof of Paige's Civic.

"Is this a general question for the car or ...?" Mattie asked, nudging Joey's knee with her own. Mattie wasn't discreet in her judgment of people's intelligence, and she historically found Lilly to be an absolute idiot.

"Well, I was mostly talking to Joey, but I guess anyone can answer," Lilly replied. Joey caught the look Lilly shot to Paige. It was obvious that Mattie's distaste of Lilly was reciprocal.

"Why Joey? Because he has a dick?" Mattie scoffed. "What difference does anatomy make? Why would you ask him a question like that and not ask the same of me?"

"I just said 'anyone can answer,'" Lilly repeated. "So that includes you."

"You said you were 'mostly talking to Joey,'" Mattie pointed out.

Lilly was about to find out what Emily and Joey already knew: Mattie didn't let things go easily.

"What difference does it make?" Lilly sighed. She turned to Paige. "You get what I was saying, right? Like, you see where I'm coming from ..."

"I heard the words that came out of your mouth," Paige laughed. "It's not like the statement was complicated."

"Why's she making it that way then?" Lilly asked as if Mattie wasn't two feet behind her.

"Why are we still talking about this?" Emily inquired. "I don't even remember the question." She tapped Joey on the top of his hand. "Do you?"

"Yeah," he replied. "The longer the conversation's going on, the more I'm wondering why I do. Do guys talk about dumb shit like this?"

"You're a guy, so you're the most qualified to answer that," Paige stated.

"I honestly don't care," Joey decided.

"About anything," Mattie added with a smirk. "You honestly don't care about anything."

"I care about things that matter," he disagreed.

"What matters to you?" Lilly questioned, craning her neck to look at Joey.

"People," Joey responded. It was an easy answer, and for the most part, it was true. He didn't get wrapped up in the dozens of superficial connections he easily made, but he definitely cared about the people he chose to surround himself with.

"Certain people," Paige corrected. "Other people,"—she clicked her tongue and shook her head—"not so much."

"Which is totally normal," Emily said. "Isn't everyone like that?"

Paige shrugged. "Maybe, but Joey is super skilled at writing people off."

"You could afford to get better at that," Lilly told Paige.

The statement earned Lilly the look of death from Paige, which was suspect. His sister was typically open about what was going on in her life. Joey made a mental note to ask about Paige's sore spot the next day.

"Well, this car ride has been sufficiently awkward," Mattie said, reaching for the pipe that was now in Emily's possession.

Joey intercepted. There was no way he was going to let them skip him. Drawing in a deep inhale, Joey allowed the smoke to burn his lungs before he coughed it out. One more hit had his thoughts muddled and his mind fuzzy.

As the car sped down I-44E toward Valley Park, Joey leaned over to Emily to open her window a bit. The small sliver ushered in a loud whooshing that filled the car, drowned out the music, and reverberated through Joey's relaxed body. The noise would have grated on him if he weren't high, but his inebriated state made him appreciate the way the air bent into a near-mechanic whirring.

Bleary-eyed and satisfied, Joey glanced at Emily and admired the way she had her hands cupped over her ears. It was like she was the monkey determined to hear no evil. Instinctively, he tuned in closer to the noise she found so offensive, listening for some satanic undertones he may have been missing. It would have made a good horror movie, messages coming from beyond through the slit of the window of a car speeding on the highway. Sloping his shoulders so he could peek out at the moon, Joey considered whether it would be demons or aliens sending their warnings. Maybe both. Demonic aliens. He'd had worse ideas.

"If demon aliens were trying to mess with us from Hell or Mars or wherever, what do you think they'd say?" Joey asked.

"What?" Paige cried as the rest of the girls laughed. "You're too high to function."

"I'm barely high," he lied. He was really fucking high, but that didn't disqualify the importance of the question.

"False," Mattie asserted. "You're most definitely super high."

"And ..." Joey challenged.

Mattie smirked and clapped her hand over Joey's mouth. "And shh."

He narrowed his eyes at her. She was insisting he ... speak no evil.

"Yo," he breathed between her fingers, hot air seeping through slits like the cold was coming through the space in the window he'd given it. The parallels were tripping him out.

"And close that, Em. We need to hotbox before we get there. We're wasting our high," Mattie directed.

Emily was making the move to do as she was told when Joey grabbed her wrist and shook his head.

"Don't," he insisted. "I like the sound."

"It's horrible," Paige chided, cracking her own window.

The release of pressure tempered the noise, but to Joey's relief, didn't cause it to dissipate completely. He'd never been so enamored by such a mundane—and irritating—sound. Though he was high as hell, he was aware that his interest was out of the ordinary.

"Where'd you get the weed?" Joey asked his sister.

"Lilly's guy."

"It's potent, huh?" Lilly grinned. She appeared to be pleased with herself, and Joey didn't fault her for her pride. Nobody in Pacific scored anything like it.

"I'm gonna need your guy's number," Joey uttered, wondering how many gallons of water it was going to take to get clean before Monday's meeting with Mr. Seaver.

"Give me your phone," Lilly said, reaching back as Joey fumbled to get his iPhone out of his pocket. "I'll put it in."

Emily ruffled Joey's hair and laughed. "There goes all your pizza money."

"No doubt," Joey agreed, fixing his messed up locks. "Quit it. I gotta look good. We're gonna run into fresh faces."

"Someone's looking to get laid," Lilly teased in a sing-song tone.

"Joey doesn't do that," Mattie tsked. "Don't act like you know him."

"And just that like that, Mattie snapped," Paige noted, widening her eyes and making a face at Joey in the rearview mirror.

"Maybe this strain makes Mattie a bitch," Emily suggested with a shrug.

"Don't start," Mattie warned.

"Well," Lilly began, "I never really needed to know about Paige's little brother's sex life, but strong work, I guess."

"Yeah, he's a virgin, so he's not 'looking to get laid,'" Mattie continued.

"Okay, okay," Joey sighed, holding his hands up. "Let's leave my dick out of this."

"I co-sign that request," Paige stated. "Nobody needs to know about anybody else's sex life."

"That sounds like confirmation that you have one to tell about," Emily noted, leaning over to waggle her eyebrows at Paige.

"And a promise I won't," Paige smirked.

"Your sister's officially more interesting than you," Mattie told Joey, who yawned in response.

"That's been a constant since his conception," Paige joked, taking the exit onto Park Valley Road. "We're almost there."

"Thank fuck," Joey groaned, rubbing his forehead. "I gotta get out of this car."

"What happened to musings about demons and aliens?" Mattie asked, squeezing Joey's knee.

"Some asshole insisted the window stay open and now shit's waning," Joey replied, chuckling at the peeved sighs that followed.

"You're that asshole," Lilly remarked.

"I'm that asshole," he confirmed, tapping his fingers against his thigh. "You guys should talk me out of the dumb shit I insist on."

Paige nodded and pursed her lips. "Oh yeah, because you're super receptive to getting talked out of things."

"He's literally the most stubborn person on the planet," Mattie agreed.

Joey rolled his eyes and Emily whispered, "You really are."

"Everyone should be quiet until we get there. Let's just have a"—he paused—"a moment of silence."

"To mourn every person who ever lost an argument to you when they were trying to talk you out of the dumb stuff you do," Mattie added.

"Amen," Joey relented, closing his eyes in an attempt to drown them all out. For the most part, he preferred to be around people, but that night he wanted to be alone in the car, focusing on whatever his mind felt compelled to zone in on. With his temperament, he doubted the party would be any fun.

He was wrong.

## 9

The party was held in one of the biggest houses in Valley Park's nicest neighborhood. Joey didn't know whose home it was or how they were able to throw a huge rager, but he didn't care. The place was packed, the music was good, and there was a line of kegs on the back deck. As far as he was concerned, it was a success.

Joey smiled at familiar faces as they walked past him. He was surprised how many kids from his school knew about the party and even more shocked that he hadn't heard about it until Paige mentioned going earlier that afternoon. It was unusual for Joey to be out of the loop, especially when it came to social events.

"Joey Mills!" a girl exclaimed, wrapping her arms around his shoulders. She hugged him tight burying her face in his chest before he had the chance to figure out who she was. Despite not knowing, he hugged her back and laughed when she started to bob to the music. "We're dancing," she decided, standing up straight.

It was Mila Mathers, the hottest cheerleader on Pacific High School's squad. She was in four of his seven classes and insisted on sitting next to him whenever he showed up to school. Her interest in him probably made the long line of dudes who drooled over her jealous as hell. He could see why. Mila was a marvel with her dark wavy hair, olive skin, and forest green eyes.

"Dancing, huh?" he grinned, letting her guide him onto the makeshift dance floor where a bunch of people were vertically fucking.

"You can, right?" Mila questioned, lifting one eyebrow as she swiveled her hips slowly and pushed flat palms down the curves of her thighs.

"I don't think too much about it," he replied, taking a drag of his cigarette and blowing the smoke over his shoulder. He dropped his free hand to the small of her back and started to move against her body.

"You just do it, hmm?" she flirted, shifting her leg between both of his. She tossed her ponytail in time with the music, licking her lips suggestively.

Glancing around the room, Joey noticed countless pairs of eyes fixed on him and his impromptu dance partner. He didn't mind the attention.

"For you," he said, handing the remainder of his cigarette to the guy dancing next to them.

"I don't smoke," the stranger objected, taking the castoff despite his protest.

Joey didn't say anything else, busying his hand in Mila's hair.

"You're so cute," Mila crooned. "So cute!"

"You're cute too," he replied easily.

"No, like, you don't understand what I'm saying; you're hot as fuck, Joey."

"I definitely understand what you're saying," he promised, leaning down to peck Mila's lightly freckled cheek.

She snaked her hand up the back of his shirt to the nape of his neck and pulled him in closer.

"I'm saying you can hit it. If you wanted to hit it right now, we could do that."

As flattered as he was by the offer, there was no way in hell it was happening. He'd kissed girls in the past, but it was nothing more than lips and tongues tangled in a completely uninspired way. There was no use considering going any further than that. "We're friends though."

Mila froze at the statement and placed her hands on her hips expectantly. "Oh c'mon."

"What?" Joey asked innocently. He couldn't help but grin at her unimpressed glare. "What?"

"We're not friends. We don't chill on the weekend."

"We're chilling right now," he pointed out. "It's Saturday."

"You know what I mean," she admonished. "If you're not into me you can tell me. I can take it."

"It's not that I'm not into you," Joey began, wishing they hadn't trodden down the treacherous path they were on. "I'm kinda involved with someone else."

"Shit," Mila uttered, looking around the room nervously. "Is she here?"

"No, uh, she's in college."

"Wow!" Mila beamed, shaking her head to show her approval. "I should've guessed. You're too cute to be single. Honestly …" she cleared her throat as if she was swallowing her words.

"What?"

"Nothing, I just," Mila paused. "I kinda thought that maybe you were gay. I mean, you never really acknowledge my flirting so … I don't know. You're cute and you dress well. Don't be insulted!"

"I'm not," Joey said easily. He ignored the way his heart was pounding more rapidly than it had been seconds before.

"Gay or insulted?"

"Either, I guess," he answered. The last thing he was going to do was stand in the middle of a Valley Park party and confess his deepest, darkest secret.

His deepest, darkest secret. He'd never found it necessary to hold back his thoughts or hold in any "secrets," but for some reason his sexuality made him react in ways he would not have otherwise.

"Well, on behalf of women in general and a girl who doesn't want to insult you, good! Honestly, there are already enough painfully cute and unattainable gay guys; I wouldn't want to add you to the mix. At least if it's because you're in a relationship, I know I have a chance. Nothing lasts forever."

"You're going to wait forever?" Joey chuckled. "Come on, Mila. You have guys banging down your door."

"Maybe I'm more concerned with banging down yours," she replied with a smirk.

"Seriously, though, I'm happy for you. Is dancing off limits or …?"

"Never," Joey answered, intertwining their fingers so he could spin Mila around.

They danced until he was way too sober to dance with her anymore. Since he clearly wasn't interested in tapping Mila, Joey excused himself to tap the keg instead.

The night was frigid, which meant the expansive backyard was nearly empty, save the faithful waiting in relatively long lines to fill their red solo cups with beer. Committed to the cause, Joey bounced a bit in an attempt to warm himself as he anticipated his turn at the keg.

"It's cold as balls out here," the guy behind him said as they endured the slight breeze that felt more like an arctic blast.

"My balls are the hottest part of my body right now," Joey said. "It's my fingers that are suffering. You should say as cold as fingers or something."

The guy chuckled as if the statement were some of Joey's top tier material. "Touché." The warmth in his laughter prompted Joey to turn around and introduce himself. He was pleased to see that the boy was handsome, with his jet-black hair and deep brown eyes.

Finagling his freezing hand out of his pocket, Joey shook the hottie's. "Joey."

"Manny."

There was a mischievous twinkle in Manny's eyes that Joey wanted to know about. After holding onto his hand for a little too long, Joey let go and shoved it back into his pocket.

"I was going to say something awful like 'I know where you can put your fingers to keep them warm,'" Manny admitted.

"And you just did," Joey smirked. He loved when a conversation went from frigid fingers to fingering assholes. "But what if I'm more worried about warming yours?"

Manny's face lit up at the prospect. "Oh, it's like that?"

Joey didn't really know what it was like, but he knew what he fantasized about. "Mm-hmm."

"Fuck," Manny grinned. "You're hot as hell, Joey."

"I'm cold as fuck," Joey disagreed as he moved toward the keg and pumped it a few times before pouring. He reached for Manny's cup and began to fill it.

"Too much head," Manny noted.

"Said no one ever."

"Do you want to go inside?" Manny asked, taking a sip of the beer Joey handed to him. "This is my friend Callie's house so we can check out her room if you're into it."

Joey didn't hesitate. "I'm into it."

It wasn't out of the ordinary for people to be attracted to Joey. He was used to garnering a good deal of interest from both sexes. His biggest issue was the size of his school and how few guys there were who he wanted to hook up with. Meeting random guys like Manny happened way too infrequently, and the last thing he was willing to do was give up the opportunity to get off with a guy who wasn't behind a phone screen.

Joey kept a safe distance from his new friend as they walked through the house, a signal that Manny read clearly. They were about to climb the stairs when Joey was intercepted by Mattie and Emily.

"Hey, there's a beer bong in the basement. You have to come try it out," Mattie said, her words slightly slurred. From the sound of it, she already had.

"We've each done two," Emily added, grabbing Joey's hand. She gave it a tug as if to pull him along with them. "You're behind, babe."

Joey glanced at Manny, who was standing a few steps up from him. "Well, I'll have to catch up soon. I gotta take a piss."

"Don't take too long," Mattie urged. "Shit's getting crazy and it's not as fun without you!"

"On it," Joey promised, grinning as his friends planted a myriad of smooches on his face. "Drunk bitches."

They laughed and flitted away as he continued up the stairway. He was looking forward to getting many more kisses. But this time he was sure the affection would be centered where it really counted. And maybe his mouth too.

## 10

It had been a while since Joey had made out with anyone, a fact that made Manny's hands clenching his ass feel that much more delicious. With his legs straddling Manny's lap, Joey rolled his hips and nipped at his new crush's plump lower lip. Fingers raking through Manny's hair, Joey alternated between delivering aggressive yanks and soft massages to his scalp. From the moans escaping Manny's mouth, Joey could tell he was into it.

"Goddamn, you're hot," Manny whispered, slipping his hands below Joey's waistband, grasping full cheeks with eager fingers. "So fucking hot."

"You're hotter," Joey mumbled into the soft dip of Manny's neck. Sucking the skin into his mouth, he nibbled and bit as Manny's breaths turned to needy pants.

"Not possible," Manny disagreed, lifting Joey into the air by his ass only to deposit him onto the bed.

Manny was shorter than Joey, but what he lacked in height, he made up for in muscle tone and confidence—a combination that had Joey desperately wanting as much of Manny as he could get. He wasn't sure he had a type, but if he did, he knew Manny was it.

Though he wasn't into people telling him what to do outside of the bedroom, Joey liked a guy who was assertive where it mattered. There was no denying his natural inclination to buck authority, but a chance to ignore the impulse was its own kind of liberation.

As soon as his back hit the mattress, Joey wrapped his legs around the tiger boy's slim waist and rolled his hips into Manny's ruts fervently.

"There are no hot gay guys at my school," Manny admitted as he went in on Joey's neck.

"Which is probably good for my grades." He halted the tongue bath to push up and look Joey in the eyes. "I wouldn't be able to pay attention if you were in my classes."

"Oh yeah?" Joey breathed, snaking his hand behind Manny's head to yank him in close for a kiss. "How would I distract you?"

"This face," Manny replied, placing his hand on Joey's cheek, "those eyes." His fingers trailed down Joey's body until they cupped the bulge growing in Joey's pants. "Holy shit."

"What?" Joey laughed, licking his lips before smacking them against Manny's again.

"What?" Manny repeated with a chuckle. "You know what."

Deciding it was unnecessary to respond, Joey guided Manny's hand below his waistband, tossing his head back as the other boy began to work on him beneath his pants. It felt good to be touched by someone else's hands for a change. Though the act itself wasn't the epitome of intimacy, it felt much more erotic than his typical solo jerk session ever had. He may have been a virgin, but he certainly wasn't touched for the very first time.

As he made out with Manny, Joey silently catalogued all the boys who had come before. In spite of his desire, the list wasn't as long as he would have liked. Manny hit the nail on the head when he referenced the lack of hot gay guys around. There was a drought, and Joey would be damned if he didn't get his dick wet whenever he could. Lucky for him, Manny seemed compelled to use his mouth for the cause.

A certain semblance of guilt crept into his mind as it continuously wandered away from the boy giving him head. Though he silently chided himself for being so disengaged, Joey couldn't control his brain's stubborn streak. For some reason, it was driven to perseverate on an exchange between Paige and Lilly earlier that night. The more he tried to push the thoughts away, the more they proved they were there to stay. Lilly had alluded to Paige having a problem cutting people out of her life, which was as much of a shock as it wasn't. His sister was strong as hell and impressively independent, but as far as Joey was concerned, she'd always given too much allowance to men—especially the one who was supposed to have raised them. He really hoped Paige didn't end up with "daddy issues" that made her accept less than what she deserved. He hoped he didn't either.

"Are you alive up there?" Manny asked, prompting Joey to push up on his elbows to get a better view of the deep espresso eyes looking down at him, perturbed.

"Barely," Joey replied, using his hand to gently coax Manny's mouth back to his member.

"You're really good. Keep going."

Manny may have been talented, but he wasn't skilled enough to demand Joey's full attention. Typically, the novelty of actually making out with a guy was enough, but whatever it was they smoked in the car had taken him to a different level of consciousness.

"You're too quiet," Manny admonished, popping his mouth off of Joey's dick. "I'm down here working, and it doesn't seem like you're into it all."

Joey cringed at the neediness in his hookup's tone. He was never desperate enough to deal with a whiny guy. It didn't matter how hot the guy was, there was no bigger turn-off than the need for empty affirmations.

"I am," Joey lied, feeling less excited by the moment. He didn't want a guy who was so hesitant. Joey needed a man who took what he wanted and made him feel *taken*. The last thing Joey was in his everyday life was subservient, but maybe that's why the concept of relinquishing all of his power was so intoxicating.

"Can you moan or something?" Manny asked, markedly exasperated by Joey's lack of participation.

"How about I take care of you?" Joey offered, repositioning himself so he was on top of his hookup. "It's better that way."

Manny grinned and Joey smirked, knowing how easy it was to refocus a guy's attention. Though his experience was limited, it was easy for Joey to see through men. It could have been because he was a man himself, but he wasn't convinced that was the case.

"Holy shit," Manny gasped, tangling his fingers in Joey's hair. "What are you doing down there?"

Whatever he'd learned watching porn. From the noises Manny was making—and the compliments he'd received in the past—Joey was convinced he was a star student.

"I'm not gonna be able to ..." Manny whispered, losing the rest of the sentence to a moan.

Joey placed a hand on Manny's trembling knee, trying to ground the guy so the night wasn't over before it really started, but it was too late.

With a throaty groan, Manny announced: "I'm cumming," as if Joey couldn't already tell. He'd finished guys off quickly before, but two minutes was a personal record.

"Wow," Joey mumbled, sitting up and wiping his mouth with the back of his hand.

"What?" Manny questioned, his cheeks tinting pink as he shifted to pull up his pants.

"Nothing. It's just that"—Joey paused, nudging his knuckle against the side of his nose—"you were making this big deal about not being around other gay guys or whatever ... I thought we'd mess around for a while, you know?"

"I mean, I can return the favor," Manny offered, "and then maybe I can, uh, be ready again."

Joey wasn't sure what he had been expecting, but it wasn't an anticlimactic hookup. Losing his virginity during a rager wasn't necessarily how he'd imagined it would happen, but Manny was cute enough and banging in a random bedroom was better than the alternative. Joey was sick of being a virgin. The more time he spent not having sex, the more he thought about sex. While he was sure it was great, he didn't want to be consumed by it anymore. He wanted to get it over with.

"We can do that," Joey decided, lying back on the bed to provide Manny access.

Though Manny put forth a valiant effort, try as he might, he couldn't carry Joey to completion. Rubbing his jaw, Manny let Joey fall out of his mouth.

"Are you getting close?" he asked, obviously aggravated by the amount of work it was taking.

"Not really," Joey admitted. "I could fuck you ..."

"Here?" Manny laughed, shaking his head. "It's not really that easy, and you're not fucking me while I'm soft. Well," he tsked, "you're not fucking me at all. You kinda alluded to the fact that you're a bottom."

"So?"

"So," Manny repeated. "Stay in your lane then."

Joey stared at Manny for a moment to see if he was going to laugh and when he didn't, Joey did.

"You're serious?"

Manny shrugged and climbed off of the bed.

"Savage," Joey chuckled, pulling up his pants.

As he watched Manny leave the room, Joey reflected on how hilarious the whole situation was and how he wished he could share the story with Paige, Mattie, and Emily.

And how the fact that he didn't feel he could wasn't funny at all.

Checking his hair in the mirror, Joey grunted at how badly Manny has messed it up. It wouldn't have bothered him as much if his balls weren't throbbing, but the combination of the two disappointments was particularly aggravating. The only way to salvage the night was to head down to the basement to do beer bongs with his friends. Though he'd only had Manny in his throat for a couple seconds, he was pretty sure he could keep the beer sliding down for the rest of the night. And on the bright side, the beer would most certainly finish him off.

## 11

Sunday was spent recuperating from Lilly's potent weed, a ton of cheap alcohol, and the hilarious hookup. The last thing Joey wanted to do was get out of bed, but Paige incessantly calling his name from her room had him begrudgingly dragging his ass across the hall.

"What?" he groaned, leaning against her door frame. When he noticed that Paige was curled up in the fetal position with a pair of sunglasses haphazardly covering her eyes, he stood up straight and walked toward the bed. "What the fuck's wrong with you?"

"It took you long enough," she chided. "Get me the puke bucket."

"Ew," he gagged, glancing at the vomit on the bed behind her. "You have to get up. You can't lay next to that."

"Getting up isn't happening."

"Well at least roll onto the floor so I can clean the sheets."

"Get the blue bucket and I will."

Sighing at the immediate task and those to follow, Joey walked down to the basement to retrieve the infamous mop pail turned go-to sick bucket. When they were younger, it was used exclusively for stomach bugs that made them too weak to get out of bed to get to the toilet, and as they got older, it was their drunk night and next morning companion.

Though it smelled like bleach, Joey still hated touching it. He carried it up the stairs holding it between his index finger and thumb as if it were contaminated by pukes of the past.

"Roll out," Joey ordered as soon as he crossed the threshold. He placed the bucket beside the bed and held his sister's hands as she hit the floor with the grace of a hippopotamus. "You're a mess," he muttered as Paige instantly wrapped her arms around the bucket and puked. He held her hair back as she went through the succession of scoffing at the disgusting act and then participating in it again.

"So nasty," Paige grunted as her sunglasses fell into the pail. "Fuck my life."

"Fuck you for drinking so much."

"You drank more than me."

"Yeah, well, I can hold my alcohol better than you," Joey said, keeping one hand wrapped around Paige's locks while reaching for the hairband lying on her nightstand. He twisted her hair into a loose topknot before attending to the bed.

Crumpling the sheets and mattress pad into a ball that protected his hands as much as possible, he tossed them into the washer before grabbing a fresh set and putting them on Paige's bed.

"Want to get back up here? It's clean."

"I'm not," she sighed, lying on the floor. "My dumb ass doesn't deserve the bed right now."

Joey looked from the bed to his sister and decided to lay next to her on the floor. She'd done the same for him enough times. Despite his reluctance, he always returned the favor. "No, you don't," he agreed, attempting to make himself comfortable. "How many beer bongs did you do?"

"Don't," Paige warned, giving a sad attempt to hold up a finger to shush Joey. "We're not talking about that."

"Can we talk about Lilly's weed then?"

"Yeah, we can talk about that."

"You've been holding out on me."

"You smoke too much weed as it is," Paige stated. "I'm not going to make it more appealing to you."

"I still smoke the mediocre shit regularly. Maybe if I smoked good stuff, I'd smoke it less often."

"Oh please," Paige laughed, holding onto her ribs. "Ugh. I'm hurting."

"This will teach you a lesson."

"What lesson is that?"

"Stop being so sloppy," Joey replied, raising his eyebrows.

"Who's sloppy?" she uttered, shooting him a dirty look. "You disappeared as usual. Your friends were freaking out looking for your shady ass."

"That's on them," Joey said easily. "I never gave them any reason to worry. I was just chilling."

"With who?" Paige pressed.

"Isn't your mouth tired from throwing up?" Joey admonished. "You should give it rest."

"Who was the girl?" Paige asked, sitting up as if she hadn't just been hunched over the puke pail.

"There wasn't a girl," Joey answered. It wasn't a lie. "You were dying two minutes ago, now all of a sudden you're a fucking meerkat."

"Keep talking," Paige grinned. "It's healing me. C'mon. I know you were hooking up. Your hair was a mess. Your hair is never a mess."

For a moment, Joey considered telling Paige the truth and sharing the strange story of Manny, but he thought better of it. An entertaining anecdote wasn't worth the change in perception it would cause. Joey didn't necessarily think his sister would think of him differently if he was gay; it wasn't like that at all. It was more that his sexuality was a secret he'd kept for so long and discussing it would be more exposure than he could cope with. He loved the attention he got from friends, family, and guys, but he wanted that interest to be based on whatever came out of his mouth rather than where he wanted to stick his dick.

As far as Joey knew, there was one other gay guy at Pacific High

School. His name was Marcus Grant, and he went to elementary school and middle school with the majority of the sophomore class. Once he came out, he was no longer known as Marcus; he was referred to as the "gay kid," as if people fully forgot who he was before his sexuality became public knowledge. He'd quickly become "oh shit, you're paired with the gay kid" or "did you see who the gay kid was sitting with at lunch today?" Joey didn't want to be demeaned to a stereotype. Though he knew his sister would never think any less of him, he was tentative to open up the flood gates and be someone who everyone knew but forgot. He was more than that. At least he hoped he was.

"There wasn't a girl," Joey repeated, partially hoping that his sister would notice his specificity. If she did, she didn't let on.

"Bullshit."

"You should worry about yourself. You're a mess."

"I am a mess," Paige agreed, slowly lowering herself to the ground. "I'm never drinking again."

Joey chuckled. "Likely story."

"As likely as your story that you weren't with a girl," Paige retorted. "That huge fucking hickey says otherwise."

Reactively, Joey raised his hand to the tender spot on his neck. "What hickey?"

"The one you're covering right now." She grinned, shaking her head from side to side. The motion must have charged her up because as soon as she did, Paige was lurching over the bucket.

"You deserved this one for being so nosy," Joey uttered, lazily tickling his sister's back.

"Nobody deserves this," Paige disagreed, spitting a few times before crumpling back down. "Nobody."

"Oh come on, we can name at least a hundred crappy people who do. We could do it right now. I'll start."

"You're really trying to avoid this conversation," Paige noted. "If I had more energy, I would be interrogating you."

"How about I interrogate you instead, then?"

"About what?" She questioned skeptically.

"Who was Lilly talking about when she said you should drop someone?"

"She didn't say that."

"She did. I don't remember her exact words but it was something like that."

"She was high."

"We all were. Since when do people lie when they're stoned?"

"It's not truth serum," Paige objected.

"Her shit was strong. It could be."

"Don't worry about it."

"So there's something to worry about?"

"There's nothing to worry about," Paige asserted.

"If there were nothing to worry about, you would've said there was nothing to worry about. You said, 'don't worry about it.'" Joey said as if he'd cracked the code.

"And then I said 'there's nothing to worry about.'"

"But you didn't say that first. You said it second."

"You'd make a good lawyer if you weren't so lazy."

"I'm not lazy," Joey stated.

"See, you'll argue anything, even facts."

"You're avoiding the conversation we're supposed to be having."

"We're not supposed to be having any conversation. I'm supposed to be hugging this bucket and hating life."

"You're doing both," Joey pointed out, gesturing to the way Paige's arms were wrapped loosely around the bottom of the bucket. "So, multi-task. Who's fucking with you?"

"Other than you right now?"

"Yup."

"It's not a big deal."

"The fact that you're being shady tells me otherwise."

"Fine. I got with this guy from school a few months ago," Paige began. "We were talking and everything was going well until, like, two weeks ago."

"From our school?" Joey interrupted.

"Yeah."

"Who is it?"

"I'm not telling you."

"Why? I'm not going to go after him and defend your honor," Joey scoffed. "What did he do?"

"You talk a lot of shit to people and he's a lot bigger than you."

Joey laughed. "And you're worried he's going to kick my ass?"

"Yup," Paige confirmed.

"What did he do?" Joey repeated.

"Nothing. He texts me to hang out once or twice a week and then ghosts me until the next text."

"So, he's using you."

"But he wasn't like this before. It just started two weeks ago," Paige explained, pushing a stray blonde lock back into the bun Joey had put her hair into.

"Did you say anything clingy?"

Paige rolled her eyes. "Like confess my undying love to him? C'mon!"

"Who knows?" Joey shrugged. "Maybe he has a girlfriend now or something?"

"Maybe," Paige muttered.

Joey narrowed his eyes at his sister. "How good is the dick that you're putting up with this crap?"

"Joey!"

"What?"

"We're not talking about that," she admonished. "Don't talk about that."

"You know what I'm going to say."

"That I can do better?"

"That you're an idiot for putting up with it. Guys will walk all over you if you let them. You're giving him an open invitation to treat you like shit. So he is. It's as simple as that," Joey said matter-of-factly.

"You're being dramatic."

"You're being every girl you judge, letting yourself get played like this."

"Can you let me puke my guts up in peace? Honestly, this conversation is making me even more nauseous."

"That's on you," Joey stated. "It would make me sick too."

"Ugh," Paige moaned, rolling her eyes. "I should have never told you."

"You basically didn't. I had to pull it out of you. If that doesn't tell you how ashamed you are of it ..." Joey paused, the assertion hitting too close to home. "Whatever." He abruptly stood up and symbolically wiped his hands. "I don't care."

"Good. There's nothing to care about."

"Great, I don't." He was about to leave the room when he turned back. "You should lay on the bathroom floor instead. I'm not cleaning the bucket."

"Who asked you to?"

"Do you need help or what?" he asked, aggravated.

"I'll crawl there if I have to."

"This strong, independent woman," Joey snarked, but he couldn't help but hope that she actually was.

He wanted better for her. Because whether or not she believed it, it was what she deserved.

## 12

It was a matter of time. Though Joey hadn't wanted to admit it, he knew it was. His weed cleanse was effective, but evidently it was no match for Lilly's marijuana. Despite chugging an additional liter to counteract the potency he had assumed of the weed, it hadn't been enough.

"You failed," Mr. Seaver reported as he took a seat behind his desk.

"That's impossible," Joey stated, garnering an aggravated look from his counselor. "What?"

"The test doesn't lie. You do."

Joey cringed. "Not often."

"Well, clearly in this case you are. What kind of trouble did you get yourself into this weekend?"

"I didn't get into any trouble this weekend. It seems like I saved all the excitement for Monday morning, huh?"

"It seems so," Mr. Seaver sighed. "What am I going to do with you?"

"I'm assuming a suspension," Joey replied, trying not to sound as blasé as he felt about the whole situation. He wished his test had been clean. Life would be less complicated if it had, but it hadn't, so there wasn't much use getting worked up over it. The worst thing that would happen was that he would get a week off from school. He skipped often but always had his mom chirping in his ear. If he wasn't supposed to attend, there wouldn't be any annoyance. It sounded good to him.

"It should be an expulsion," Mr. Seaver said, shaking his head with disappointment. "You don't remember me telling you another infraction would lead to expulsion?"

Joey vaguely recalled the threat but shrugged in response.

"I've told you that consequence in nearly every conversation we've had in the last four months," Seaver chided, tapping his pen anxiously against the file lying on his desk. "I can't go to bat for you."

"I would never ask you to," Joey promised. It was a juggling act to express his disinterest while attempting not to come across as disrespectful. As much as he couldn't stand the school and its policies, Joey liked Mr. Seaver. Things would have been worse if he'd had a dick for a counselor.

"So, that's it, then? You have no fight in you? You don't want to plead your case?"

"It sounds like a done deal," Joey responded, confused. "I don't know what you want me to say?"

"I want to see that it affects you, that you're bothered by an imminent expulsion," Mr. Seaver cried. "I want to know you give a shit about the fact that you're at a crossroads that can change the trajectory of your entire life. I want to know you feel anything."

Joey sat wide-eyed, shocked by the outburst. "You cursed."

"That's what you took from what I just said?" the counselor breathed, staring at Joey as if he were either an alien or an imbecile. "You have to be kidding me!"

"I hear everything you're saying," Joey assured. "I hear it and I don't see it that way, I guess."

Mr. Seaver let out a stuttering exhale. "How do you see it, Mills? Tell me. I'm actually intrigued."

"I mean, worst comes to worst, I can always do one of those online high schools or take the GED. It doesn't matter how you do it as long as you get it done. Or," Joey paused, "I could not finish school at all. I have a good job. I can make a living waiting tables."

"And that would be enough for you? You're a bright kid."

"So? My mom's smart and she's a waitress. There's nothing wrong with having a career where you work hard and do what needs to be done to earn money," Joey replied, defensively. "The problem with people is they think everyone has to be like them. You think I should go and get a wall full of degrees like you," Joey accused, gesturing wildly toward the frames hanging to the right of the desk. "Maybe I'm different than you and everyone else here. I'm okay with that."

Mr. Seaver sat motionless, clearly dumbfounded by Joey's argument and the ease with which he presented it. "I don't ..."

"You don't what?" Joey challenged, filling in the blanks in his own head: *"know what to say," "know what to do with a kid like you," "understand the person you are or anything about you."*

"I don't know what the school board will decide. It's supposed to be zero tolerance after the first offense, but you've already had several and they've let you slide."

"Why?" Joey wondered. "Why would they do that?"

"I have no idea," Mr. Seaver admitted. "Maybe it was that you looked innocent, seemed contrite, or my recommendations to give you another shot."

"Are you going to do that again?"

"Make a recommendation to give you another chance?"

Joey nodded. "Yeah." He wasn't sure what answer he wanted to hear. The path of least resistance would be for Seaver to go to bat for him and his mother to sleep easier for at least a few more nights.

"Do you want me to?" Mr. Seaver questioned. "You just served me a diatribe about how little school matters to you."

"It matters to my mom," Joey stated as if that was reason enough for the counselor to advocate for a kid who just told him he didn't care about school.

"If it doesn't matter to you, you'll have another infraction. It's just a matter of time. You'll let her down. You'll let me down. You'll let yourself down."

"I don't know what to tell you," Joey replied. "It's not like weed is the most important thing in my life. If I want to stop smoking it, I can."

"Do you want to?"

"Fuck no," Joey laughed. "That should be pretty fucking obvious."

Mr. Seaver closed his eyes and took a deep breath as if trying to summon patience that was quickly fleeting. "If weed isn't the most important thing in your life, what is?"

"My family, my friends," Joey answered as if the question was ludicrous. "I'm not an ingrate. I give a shit about the people in my life."

"I try not to assume. It's easy for you to be cold and unaffected by so many other things you should care about," Mr. Seaver stated.

"What compares to the people you love?" Joey inquired. The question wasn't rhetorical, but Mr. Seaver treated it like it was. "Seriously," Joey pressed.

"Sometimes I wonder if your head's screwed on straight, and you go ahead and make statements like that," the counselor rubbed his temples in a circular pattern. "I don't know what to do with statements like that and results like this," he confessed, dropping a hand to hold up the litmus paper. "Where do we go from here?"

"I think that's up to the school board."

"It sure is," Mr. Seaver agreed. "I need to call your mom and tell her what's going on."

"Can't I just tell her in person? I'll go over to the restaurant."

"Absolutely not. That's not how things work," Mr. Seaver answered. "You're fifteen. You don't get to deliver information like this on your own."

"Alright. I'll let you be the bearer of bad news then," Joey replied, sinking lower in the chair. He wasn't looking forward to how loud the night was going to be. There was no doubt in his mind that Bridget was going to go on an epic rant as soon as he got in front of her. He didn't blame her. He would be pissed if he was his kid too.

Joey watched as Mr. Seaver dialed his mother's number. There were pangs and pricks of guilt while he waited for his mother's day to be ruined. It wasn't that he wanted to torture Bridget with his decisions, it was more that he didn't feel compelled enough to protect her from them.

Listening to Seaver's side of the conversation, it became obvious that the counselor was going to, once again, recommend that the board show mercy to Joey, a favor he knew he didn't deserve. Perhaps it was Bridget's frustration that drove Mr. Seaver to the decision. Joey could hear her sighs and groans loud and clear from the receiver of the phone.

"Your mother is not at all happy," Mr. Seaver reported as he hung up.

"I didn't think she would be."

"She kept repeating something about your 'dumbass cleanse.' Care to explain?"

"I really don't," Joey replied, holding his hands up in surrender. "It's definitely not something you want to know."

"Not something I want to know or not something you want to tell me?" Seaver attempted to clarify.

"Honestly, not something you want to know. I'll tell you, but you're not gonna want to hear it."

"Try me," Mr. Seaver decided, leaning back in his chair and crossing his arms over his chest. "It's 9:30am, and it's already been a crappy day. Do you think you'll make it worse?"

"For you or myself?" Joey questioned, matching the counselor's posture.

"I'm going with both on this one."

"You're probably right," Joey conceded. "So, there's this way to trick the test."

"What test? The drug test?"

Joey nodded his head slowly. "Yup."

"Impossible," Mr. Seaver exclaimed. "Absolutely impossible."

"Or, highly fucking possible," Joey asserted. "I've literally done it for every single test. The only reason I didn't pass this one is because I smoked some crazy strain on Saturday night."

"No way."

"I swear. All you have to do is chug, like, two gallons of water and then some soda to give your piss some color."

"And you did that every time?"

"Every time," Joey confirmed. He studied the counselor's stunned face. "I probably messed up the chances that you'll speak up for me, huh?"

"Do you care if you did?" Seaver challenged.

Joey knew he should have said yes and showed how much he wanted the good words, but he couldn't be so disingenuous. "My mom will care."

"And ...?" Mr. Seaver dug.

"And she's annoying, but she's a good person."

"That sounds like someone else I know," Mr. Seaver relented with a click of his tongue.

Joey sat quietly, but it wasn't lost on him that the counselor thought he was an okay guy.

## 13

The air seemed colder as Joey walked home from school for what could have been the last time. Maybe it was the speed with which he was traipsing, not finding it necessary to rush toward his mother's anger. Or perhaps it was the bone-chilling realization that he really had fucked up. Everything he'd said to Mr. Seaver was the truth. He didn't particularly care about school or think getting kicked out was that big of a deal, but he knew Bridget was going to lose her mind. He didn't particularly blame her, especially after the succession of stresses he'd caused her in his decade and a half of life. It was one more thing for her already anxious mind to worry about.

Joey was thankful for Steve. Without him, Bridget would have spiraled a long time before. She'd been through more than one person should have to deal with in thirty-three years. She was strong, but she shouldn't have had to be as much of a soldier as she was. Steve was solid in a way Joey's father could have never been, a way Joey was sure he could never be either.

There were some people who were meant to care for others, people who held compassion in their core. Steve was a protector without diminishing Bridget's capability to look out for herself. They had found each other at a turbulent time, yet he never held the circumstances against her, never questioned her loyalty, and in turn, she never doubted his. Though Joey never discussed it with anyone, he respected the hell out of their relationship. He liked to give Bridget shit as often as possible, but he couldn't fault her for Steve. Marrying her husband was the best thing Bridget had ever done. Joey was sure his mother would say the same. She certainly wouldn't say it was her children, especially after Paige's horrible two-day hangover that had turned her into a raging bitch and Joey's pending expulsion.

He needed a cigarette. Kneeling on the side of the road, Joey searched his backpack for the two cigarettes and lighter he hid in a secret pouch for emergencies. Lighting one up, he let the filter rest on his lips as he zipped his bag up and slid the strap over his shoulder. He was barely a few feet down the street when his nicotine-calmed stroll was interrupted by an insistent buzzing in his back pocket.

Looking at the screen, Joey saw nearly a dozen texts from his group chat with Mattie and Emily.

*Emily (10:04am): Where's Joey?*

*Emily (10:04am): Joey, where are you?*

*Emily (10:04am): Mattie, have you seen him? If he's not in by now, Mr. Seaver is going to have his ass.*

*Mattie (10:04am): Maybe he's skipping. It wouldn't be the first time. Why are you freaking out?*

*Emily (10:05am): He's been on a streak. He hasn't missed in two weeks.*

*Mattie (10:05am): No way.*

*Emily (10:05am): It's true.*

*Mattie (10:05am): All the more reason for him not to show. You know he can't keep that shit up.*

*Mattie (10:05am): It's against his nature.*

*Joey (10:06am): What's my nature?*

*Emily (10:06am): He lives.*

*Mattie (10:06am): Inconsistent.*

*Joey (10:06am): My nature is inconsistency?*

*Mattie (10:06am): Confirmed.*

*Emily (10:07am): Co-signed.*
*Joey (10:07am): Well, Seaver will probably agree.*
*Emily (10:07am): What happened?*
*Joey (10:08am): My test came back dirty.*
*Mattie (10:08am): Fuck*
*Emily (10:08am): Shit*
*Joey (10:08am): Yeah. I guess Lilly's weed was too much for my process.*
*Mattie (10:09am): I literally hate that girl so much.*
*Emily (10:09am): It's totally not her fault.*
*Joey (10:09am): Not at all.*
*Mattie (10:09am): Well, I hate her anyway. This just adds to it.*
*Emily (10:10am): What did Bridge say?*
*Joey (10:10am) On my way home now...*
*Mattie (10:10am): She's gonna be piiiissed. Not looking forward to working with you two tonight.*
*Joey (10:11am): She already knows. It'll be fine.*

It would be. No matter how much steam Bridget blew off, she'd get over it. She always did.

A gust of wind had Joey picking up his pace. A storm was coming, and he feared it would be more of a force than he was willing to weather.

Jogging down the driveway, Joey entered the code into the garage door pad and sighed when he saw Steve's truck. He hadn't even considered the chance that his stepfather might be home. If he'd had a tactic it would have had to shift to deal with Steve, but he hadn't thought that far ahead. He should have. It wasn't that he was intimidated by Steve, it was more that he wanted his respect because it wasn't promised or laced with the unconditional love his mother's was. Steve wasn't a fair-weather father, but Joey knew he wasn't down for him the way Bridget was. Nobody could be. There was something next level about a mother's love. Even through all of their issues, Joey knew that was fact.

"Wait, they actually sent you home?" Bridget asked as soon as Joey entered the kitchen.

"Fuck," he muttered, drawing skeptical looks from his mother and Steve, who seemed to have been enjoying a leisurely morning of coffee and the paper before his arrival.

"I thought it was a warning," Bridget sighed, folding up the entertainment page to turn her attention to Joey. "Mr. Seaver made it sound like this was something that could be handled."

"Maybe it can be," Joey replied, opening the refrigerator to drink orange juice directly from the carton. "It's not that big of a deal. He didn't make it a big deal to you, so it's not, right?"

"Yet, it's"—Steve glanced at the clock on the microwave—"10:35am and you're standing in the kitchen chugging juice like an animal rather than sitting in class."

"I'm not denying that I got in some trouble," Joey said as he busied himself with searching the refrigerator for nothing in particular.

"I'm shocked," Bridget deadpanned. "Usually you try to deny facts."

"What's the bottom line?" Steve asked.

"Mom probably already told you, but I guess my drug test came back positive for weed," Joey answered. "Which is weird considering I did my typical shit to get rid of the traces."

A loud groan had Joey standing up straight to look at his mom.

"I can't get over what a dumb thing it is to get in trouble for. You knew you were going to get tested."

Joey held his hands out as if presenting the obvious. "I've beat the test every single time, Mom. This was a total fucking fluke. I even told Seaver that."

"Oh, that's great," Bridget said sarcastically, rubbing her furrowed forehead as Steve tickled her back soothingly. "And what did he say about that?"

"I mean, he was surprised."

"You're not an idiot," Steve stated, "but goddamn if you don't act like one sometimes."

"Most of the time," Bridget corrected. "So after telling your counselor that you've been consistently cheating the system that's been put in place to keep you clean, he said ..."

"Honestly, I stopped paying attention," Joey admitted. "Something about petitioning the school board."

"And this isn't a big deal?" Bridget scoffed.

"What did he say to you?" Joey retorted. "You said it seemed like things were going to be handled. It sounded like that to me, too."

"Was anybody paying attention to this guy while he was explaining the ramifications?" Steve wondered.

Bridget sighed. "I was paying attention, but all of the phone calls end up sounding the same."

Joey clapped and nodded his head emphatically. "Exactly. That's exactly what I'm saying." He waved his arms in the air. "It starts to blend together."

"We're not bonding over this," Bridget tsked. "I'm angry, Joey. What if this is an expulsion? What are you going to do then?"

"He did mention expulsion," Joey recalled. "Did he talk about it with you?"

Steve regarded Bridget expectantly as she shrugged guiltily.

"I was half asleep," she defended. "This is the first phone call home I've gotten this week, but it isn't the first phone call home."

"It's only Monday," Steve reminded.

"I'm just saying it all ..." Bridget paused.

"Blends together," Joey filled in. "That's exactly what I'm saying."

"I'll have to call him back," Bridget told her husband. "I didn't expect to have a kid home today. I'm worried it's a bigger deal than I thought."

"It will be fine," Joey said easily. "I'm not worried."

"Tell me something you are worried about," Steve suggested. "It would be good to compare the two."

"Honestly, I'm not worried about anything," Joey confessed. "So ..."

"So that's weird!" Bridget cried. "What are you going to do if you can't go to school with your friends anymore? Wouldn't that suck?"

Joey shrugged. "I guess so, but I could always do online school or go to another school and make more friends. It's not, like, hard to make friends or whatever. You just say something like 'I fucking hate school' and they're like 'No way, I do too.' One thing leads to another, and you're rolling blunts behind the bleacher during biology class. That's literally all it takes."

Bridget and Steve stared at Joey with their jaws resting squarely on the kitchen table.

"He doesn't get it," Steve mumbled.

"Not at all," Bridget confirmed.

"Maybe you guys don't get it," Joey replied, giving them a cheeky grin. "Have you ever taken that into consideration?"

With that, Joey climbed the stairs to his bedroom, content that the conversation had gone better than expected. He breathed easy as he got ready to take a nap before his night shift at D'Antonio's. There was a game that night, and he knew the place would be a zoo. It didn't bother him though. He was looking forward to the tips. It was a lot simpler to deal with hard work when he knew the reward for it was money. What did school give him besides a headache? When it came down to it, Pacific High could never compete with cash.

People wanted to knock ambition when it didn't fit their vision, but as far as Joey was concerned, he saw everything clearly—and his eyes deserved a rest.

## 14

Walking into D'Antonio's on Monday night felt strangely permanent in a way that it had never felt before. Joey knew it was his brain attempting to wrap itself around his mouth's proclamation that he would be fine working at the pizza parlor for the rest of his life. It wasn't that he wouldn't be okay with a future in food service, it was more that the concept of any future at all was daunting. He didn't want to look forward when he wasn't even fully aware of what was going on in the present. He had never had aspirations to go to college, but he could see the appeal. It was a great way for teenagers to extend their youth and shirk responsibility for another four years. Sure, they had to go to class or whatever, but the majority of their time was spent getting drunk, high, and laid on money the government loaned them. The lucky ones had parents who were wealthy enough to take care of the bill. He could see the appeal, but what it would take to get there was beyond his bullshit threshold.

Still, if Joey stopped and allowed himself to think about what he wanted out of his life, catering to customers' hungry stomachs wasn't it. For the most part, waiting tables was enjoyable, but he couldn't imagine doing it for as long as Bridget had. It took an immense amount of patience he knew he would never be able to muster long-term. Plus, he knew that somehow he wanted to be rich, not as much for the money itself, but for the power that came with it. He didn't want to answer to anyone. He wanted the freedom that only wealth could afford. Joey wasn't going to make bank working as a waiter in a family-run hometown spot. And food workers were forced by the nature of their jobs to answer to everyone for the extent of their shifts. Basically, the more he thought about it, the more Joey was convinced he needed to become independently wealthy, stat.

He didn't want the restaurant to feel as stifling as it did. The fact that it was by far his best way to earn a paycheck should have made it more appealing, but the incident earlier that day added weight to things that had been otherwise light. There was no doubt in Joey's mind that he would get kicked out of his house if he was expelled from school *and* lost or quit his job. D'Antonio's remained proof to his mother that he could keep his shit together enough to be a somewhat functional member of society. He didn't like expectations, especially when he knew he had to live up to them, at least for a little while.

"Look who showed up to work!" Mattie teased, clapping as Joey strode into the kitchen. "He is risen."

"He's Jesus now?" Ernie admonished, shaking his head in disapproval. "That's sacrilege if I ever heard it."

"Jesus served people food and was constantly in trouble," Joey smirked. "I get the comparison. It's kinda brilliant."

"You two are kind of demented," Ernie stated, shoving a pie into the oven. "A new brand of trouble?"

"For Jesus or me?" Joey questioned, leaning over the pass to grab a garlic knot from Ernesto's station.

"I know all about him," the cook assured. "I'm asking about you."

"Same shit, different day," Joey replied, mouth half full of the appetizer.

Ernesto shook his head in a display of disapproval. "Bridget must be thrilled."

Joey shrugged as Mattie draped her arm over his shoulders.

"It was barely his fault," she explained. "This girl smoked us out with some wicked weed. There was no accounting for it."

"He could have *not* smoked the weed," Sal offered, earning perplexed looks from Mattie and Joey.

"That's not the point," Mattie stated. "The point is this bitch gave us, like, a crazy-ass strain and now Joey's paying the price."

"For his bad decision," Sal added. "It happens."

"What's the price?" Ernesto questioned. "What are you paying?"

"I guess I'm facing a possible expulsion," Joey replied. "I doubt it will happen."

"Oh yeah?" Ernesto wondered with the twinkle of amusement in his eyes. "Why's that?"

Joey shrugged again. "I don't know. It's just a feeling."

"That's the feeling you get when you've gotten away with too much," Krista informed the crew as she entered the kitchen. "This cutie has gotten away with way too much," she claimed, squeezing Joey's cheeks. "It's the benefit of having a baby face. People excuse the adult-level mistakes you make."

"It sounds like you're speaking from experience," Joey teased, returning the affectionate act to his boss. "I'm sure you got away with a good amount in your day."

"In my day," Krista cackled. "You make it sound like I'm way older than I am."

"Good job, bro," Ernie chuckled.

"He's got a way of with getting himself in the dog house too," Sal muttered loud enough for everyone to hear.

Joey wasn't sure how old Krista was but guessed she was a few years older than Bridget. Generally, he didn't give much thought to people's ages. They were either interesting or not. The year they were born had nothing to do with it.

Though the circumstances over the years had weighed on Joey's relationship with his mother, there were many times when he could have safely said she was his best friend. People may have argued that it was because Bridget was a young mom and they had grown up together, which was partially the truth. Despite their narrow age gap,

Bridget had always been a mother. She had to be because if she weren't, Paige and Joey wouldn't have had a solid parent. Bridget's actions had taught Joey that when they needed to, people had the capacity to rise to monumental heights. He didn't know if he could, but his mother had, and that was inspiring as hell even when he didn't want to let it be. Joey wondered if he would be able to sacrifice the way Bridget had if he were in the same situation. Whenever he got caught in that train of thought, Joey ended up relieved that being a teen parent wasn't in the cards for him. What a blessing it was not to want to stick his dick in a vagina.

"I didn't mean it that way," Joey promised, hugging Krista tightly. Typically, he would have laughed the comment off and expected Krista to do the same, but Joey certainly didn't need to take any chances pissing off another authority figure. He was on a role. Between Mr. Seaver, Steve, and his mother, Joey didn't have the energy to juggle another bothered adult.

"I'm assuming this cuddlefest means my son is somehow positioning himself for forgiveness," Bridget sighed as she hurried into the kitchen. She focused her attention on the cooks. "Guys, I need a pepperoni pie on the fly for table six. They said the last one was too greasy."

"It's pepperoni pizza," Sal stated. "It's the epitome of grease."

"Blot it with a napkin or something," Bridget suggested, shaking her head at the request. "I don't know."

"Put less cheese and take a napkin to the dip in the pepperoni when it comes out of the oven," Krista suggested.

"I want somebody to take me in a back alley and shank me if I ever get like that when I'm older," Mattie said wide-eyed. "That's next level."

"Completely," Joey agreed. "I'll shank you if I need to."

"That's a true friend," Mattie grinned. "I appreciate your willingness to off me."

"I'm a humanitarian," Joey joked, moving across the room so he could wrap his arms around Bridget's waist and rest his chin on her shoulder. "Mama."

"Don't 'mama' me," she tsked, refusing to turn around.

"I'm not perfect."

Bridget laughed sardonically. "No shit."

"Imagine how boring I would be if I were. I keep things interesting," Joey said. "You have to give me that."

"Every day with you has always been an adventure," Bridget agreed in a way that promised she found it less charming than Joey wished to present it.

"Steve and I were supposed to have a laid-back date day, and it was ruined by the fact that I couldn't talk about anything else besides your bullshit."

"You would've rather talked about his bullshit?"

Bridget turned around and looked up into Joey's eyes, unamused. "You know he doesn't—" she began, but she was cut off by Joey holding his hands up in surrender.

"You know I'm kidding."

"Jokes are supposed to be funny, and you're not funny at all right now," Bridget chided.

"Honestly, you're annoying me."

Rolling his eyes, Joey left the suddenly quiet kitchen to head out to the dining room. There was probably already a table of hungry patrons waiting for him. At least they would be relieved to see his face.

Joey tried not to let people's disappointment in him affect him. If he took it to heart, he would be living every day striving to be better than he had the ability to be. He'd made himself fine with being a wildcard long before. There was no way he was going to allow the gravity of the situation to change his outlook or his approach toward life. It was probably the Taurus stubbornness his family always teased him about that put the preservation of his viewpoints and the actions that accompanied them above what would have made his life easier. It was probably a character flaw that he was ready and willing to fuck with his outcomes in order to do it his way, but he was well aware that he was a flawed character to begin with. And that kept the expectations low.

## 15

Abstaining from smoking weed was manageable, but it wasn't what Joey wanted to do. He'd spent so much time getting high that not being on an alternate plane felt stranger than he was willing to admit. It was a contradiction that life was both duller and more stressful when he wasn't inebriated. He wasn't used to dealing with the level of emotion a lucid mind experienced, and he didn't like it. Doubt that Joey rarely felt had somehow crept in, causing him to wonder if he had fucked things up beyond repair and then admonish himself for worrying about something that wouldn't have bothered him in the past. The long list of non-traditional options he'd thought of for his education—or lack thereof—wasn't as appealing as staying at Pacific High School. The place might have been lame, but Joey got away with murder there. His teachers barely cared if he showed up to class, and every day he chose to go to school was like the social event of the season. It would be strange not to be with the cohort he had matriculated with since elementary.

Of course, there were benefits to enrolling in an online school and even more advantages to not going to school at all. The idea of waking up in the morning and not having to deal with math he'd never use or some bullshit poems from Shakespeare sounded like a dream. Though he skipped a lot of school, the expectation still remained that he be there. He didn't want to live up to societal standards of who he was supposed to be. How stifling it was to be indebted to institutions that weren't worthy of the esteem they garnered.

As far as Joey was concerned, the whole education system was backward. Teachers were forced to teach to tests that measured students' ability to memorize information rather than focus on what really mattered. He knew his interest in art and beauty would get him further than a cursory knowledge of physics. He needed to move to Paris, Milan, or some other European country that gave a shit about the important things in life. He needed to be immersed in culture in a way he could never be in Pacific, Missouri. Everyone in his town thought fashion was whatever hit the racks at Abercrombie and Fitch. The only education he wanted was one that high school wouldn't give him. He needed to know the world. And if not all of it, the gorgeous parts would do.

Joey wondered if he would have been "out" if he lived in another city, state, or country. Had he subconsciously stayed in the closet because walking out of it and into small-minded Missouri was an unattractive prospect? Would the early crushes he'd had on other boys have been less confusing if he'd been reared in a place where it wasn't shocking or out of the ordinary to be gay? It was strange to consider all that could have changed by a change in geography. Maybe somehow he would be different too. Joey wondered if he would like himself as much as he did if his circumstance or location had made him somebody else. Would he even be able to recognize himself?

"It's weird not smoking," Emily noted as she, Mattie, and Joey reclined on the couch in Mattie's parents' basement. "Like, we're sitting here watching trashy reality TV, and we're not stoned."

"It's inhumane," Mattie sighed. "How often are we all off from work nowadays?"

"You guys can smoke," Joey reminded them, annoyed at the continuation of the same conversation they had been having for the last hour. "I told you. Smoke. It won't bother me."

It was a lie. It would bother him, but there was no way in hell he'd admit it. He wouldn't allow anything to make him look weak enough to need it, even something he enjoyed as much as marijuana.

"Bullshit," Emily scoffed. "We know you better than that."

"Then stop fucking talking about it," Joey laughed, nudging his friend in the ribs playfully.

"Just pack a bowl and get it over with."

"No way. We're ride or die," Mattie promised. "If you can't smoke, we won't smoke."

Joey rolled his eyes and leaned forward to open the bag of Cheetos on the coffee table. He shoved a handful into his mouth and grumbled, "That's stupid."

"Do you know what's stupid?" Mattie began. "Lilly."

"It would be 'do you know *who's* stupid,'" Emily corrected.

"Do you know who's annoying?" Mattie asked, sending Joey and Emily into a fit of giggles.

"Do I even need to say it?"

"You don't need to say it," Joey grinned. "But you're going to."

"I am," Mattie confirmed with a smirk. "Emily's annoying."

"Thanks for clearing that up," Emily said. "I was kind of confused."

"Get with it," Mattie teased. "Seriously though, I can't stand that girl."

"Lilly?" Joey questioned.

"Lilly," Mattie affirmed. "She's the worst."

"What did this girl ever do to you? You've been on the warpath for weeks," Emily tsked.

"Weeks?" Mattie echoed, her face making it clear she was unconvinced. "Days at most. Don't act like she's important enough to take up my energy or brain space."

"You've been pretty pressed by her recently," Joey reasoned, clicking his tongue at Mattie's exaggerated contrary reaction. "Are you really going to try to deny it?"

Mattie shook her head. "I can admit it, but *hello*." She waved her hands in front of Joey's face. "She's the reason why you got in trouble."

"Do your arms hurt from that stretch?" Emily asked, placing her hands on Mattie's elbows with mock concern.

"Joey's been smoking nonstop for months. One night messing with her shit and he's facing expulsion," Mattie argued. "That's shit. She should've warned him or something."

"I'm sure she doesn't know anything about my weekly dates with Seaver, and even if she does, it's not on her," Joey disagreed. "It's on the school."

Emily chuckled. "Oh, that's who's responsible?"

"If they didn't worry about shit that doesn't matter, I wouldn't be dealing with this situation at all," Joey reasoned, his theory earning a glare from Mattie. "What? Where's the lie?"

"It's not so much about lies as it is about delusions," Emily replied. "Our girl has a vendetta and you have a victim complex."

Shared glances with Mattie convinced Joey that Emily's statements had aggravated her as much as they bothered him. Typically, he loved Emily's ability—and willingness—to call things out, but he was too sober to appreciate the savage realism. He knew what the possible outcomes were for the infractions, and the last thing he needed was added tension around the situation.

"Are you sure it won't bother you?" Mattie asked, pulling a baggie of pot out of her back pocket. "If it does, we won't."

"We shouldn't," Emily whispered, staring at Mattie as if she was trying to pass subliminal notes to her.

"You're acting like I'm an addict," Joey chided, downing more Cheetos before lighting a cigarette. "It's making shit more uncomfortable than it would be if you just got high."

"We'll stop holding off, then," Mattie decided. "If you're cool with it, we'll stop worrying."

"There's no need to worry," Joey stated. "Fucking smoke a bowl."

He hated himself for becoming increasingly angry as Mattie prepped the bowl. He wasn't supposed to be so smitten by a substance. He had spent his childhood witnessing his father be dependent on drugs he didn't want to succumb to. He didn't want the same fate.

Joey knew his sobriety was compelling him to overthink things. Fleeting thoughts became persistent mantras in a clear mind. Yet, no matter how loud his head was, Joey's obstinance was louder. A quiet moment allowed him to recalibrate and rebrand his anxious thoughts. If he ordered his body to resist, it would. Something that took precedence hours before would fade into oblivion as soon as Joey decided he didn't care about it anymore. The ability to forget what others were plagued to remember was the benefit of a stubborn soul. If he wanted it gone, it would be. There was no craving or affliction stronger than Joey's resistance of weakness. He just needed to remind himself of that.

Plumes of smoke filled the air as his friends got high. In order to avoid the pull of the pot, Joey made a concerted effort to focus his attention on cheese puffs. One after another, he shoved the snack into his mouth, wondering if people could become addicted to weed. There had to have been research done on the matter. Joey was sure it was somewhere, but he didn't have the energy or wherewithal to look. Instead, he watched his friends partake in an act he wished he was able to. Were they as taken by the drug as he was? Maybe it was good that his circumstances dictated that he lay off the shit for a while, if only to prove that he could.

"You know what I else I hate about her?" Mattie began, garnering groans from Joey and Emily.

"You're possessed," Emily sighed, shaking her head.

"She's so fake," Mattie continued, seemingly unfazed by her friends' disinterest. "And argumentative!"

"If she was fake, she wouldn't be argumentative. She would just agree with whatever anyone else said to please them," Emily reasoned, blowing smoke toward Mattie's face.

"That's totally not the case," Mattie disagreed.

"It kinda is," Joey interjected. "I mean, think about it. We're the realest motherfuckers around and all we do is argue."

"Man, we must be really fun to hang out with," Emily laughed, resting her head on Joey's shoulder.

"The best," Joey agreed.

That was one thing he was sure of.

## 16

Typically, two days off from work would have been appealing to Joey, but the downtime coupled with his school drama proved to be more anxiety-inducing than leisurely. The new sense of worry he had been dealing with seemed to increase by the day. It was so pervasive that Joey had to find ways to burn off the nervous energy, one of which was running up and down the stairs.

Physical fitness had never been a priority to him. He was thankful for his naturally slim body and hadn't found it necessary to build muscle on his thin frame. When he flipped through magazines, Joey knew that the guys plastered on the pages modeling the high-end looks resembled him. He wasn't cocky, but he was convinced that when he lost his baby face, he could compete with them. Maybe that was what he would do, move to Los Angeles or New York City and try to break into the industry. Nobody cared what a guy did in high school if he could sell garments to the few who could afford them and make the masses who couldn't covet them. Joey wanted to make people want things. He wanted to make people want *him*. He'd spent too much of his life being a lunch table orator. He needed a bigger audience.

Perhaps he needed to start painting again, to give strokes of acrylic on canvas the voice and reach he found it difficult to gain in Pacific. The more time he spent in limbo, the more Joey was compelled to figure out what the hell he would do if he was expelled from school. D'Antonio's was the forever option, but Joey feared Mr. Seaver was correct, that it wouldn't be enough for him. His dreams were growing greater than his ambition, which was a problem he wasn't convinced he had the energy to face.

"Again?" Bridget asked, side-stepping Joey as he continued to ascend the stairs. "I've never seen you so into your fitness."

"I'm not into my fitness. I'm crawling out of my fucking skin," Joey replied breathlessly.

Bridget stopped on the landing, watching as Joey turned at the top to head back down.

"What?" he questioned, confused by his mother's expression.

"I've also never seen you so nervous about the outcome of a school board meeting."

"I'm not nervous," Joey protested, pausing beside his mother. "Do I really seem nervous to you?"

"Um, yes," Bridget replied matter-of-factly. "You just said you're crawling out of your skin."

"That's not because I'm nervous," Joey asserted. "It's because I'm bored."

"I have plenty of things for you to do if you're bored," Bridget stated as she walked down the stairs. "You can start by cleaning your room. It's an absolute pigsty. After you handle that, you can move on to the garage. Sort through all of your skateboards, bikes, whatever you have in there with wheels, and decide what you're not using so we can donate them."

"You're doing a lot of talking right now, Ma, and I'm not doing a lot of listening," Joey said, smirking when his mother turned to glare at him.

"You think you're a funny guy, don't you?" Bridget sighed.

"You think I'm pretty funny too," Joey asserted, lifting his eyebrows and smiling sweetly at Bridget. "I'm definitely your most clever child."

"Paige disagrees," Bridget retorted, giving Joey's signature smirk right back to him.

"She does," Paige confirmed, wrapping Bridget in a hug. "You're so short."

"Petite," Bridget corrected. "Where did you come from?"

"Somewhere in this vicinity," Paige answered, waving her hand in front of their mother's lower stomach.

Bridget laughed and shoved Paige away.

"See. Clever," his sister noted, smiling up at Joey. "How are your laps going?"

"Eh," Joey sighed.

"I'm going over to Lilly's if you want to come," Paige offered.

"Cool. Let me get dressed," Joey replied.

"Really?" Bridget huffed. "What about all the tasks I just gave you?"

"I told you I wasn't listening," Joey reminded, giving his mother one last grin before heading to his room to get changed.

Pulling on a grey hoodie and a pair of jeans, Joey assessed himself in front of the full-length mirror behind his door. He certainly wasn't straight out of the pages of Vogue, but it was fine for an afternoon with Paige and Lilly. He attempted to smooth down the wild bedhead he'd been sporting since earlier that morning, and when the effort proved to be futile, Joey accepted defeat and threw on a worn-in red snapback.

Paige was waiting in her car with the passenger window rolled down and an unlit cigarette between her fingers. Climbing into the seat, Joey eyed his sister suspiciously.

"What's this all about?" he asked skeptically, placing the filter between his lips. "You're being uncharacteristically good to me."

"I'm always good to you," Paige remarked, lighting the cigarette for Joey. "You're just too fickle to notice."

"I'm not fickle at all," Joey contended, not entirely sure what the word meant. He made a mental note to look it up later. "You're fickle."

"I'm the polar opposite of fickle."

"And what would that be?" Joey inquired, fishing for context.

"Exactly what I am," she answered vaguely, beginning to back her Civic out of the driveway.

Joey considered continuing the conversation but thought better of it. Everybody teased him for his stubbornness when, by Joey's estimate, Paige was way worse than him. "What's going on with that guy?"

"Which guy?"

Taking his cigarette between his fingers so he could gape wide-mouthed at his sister, Joey asked, "There's more than one?"

Paige laughed. "No."

"Mm-hmm," Joey hummed, unconvinced and impressed. "Paige the Player. I see how it is."

Paige rolled her eyes, but her smirk made it obvious that she was amused by the nickname.

Clearing his throat, Joey persisted. "But really, what happened with that asshole you told me about during your epic hangover last week?"

"There's nothing new to report."

"Have you talked to him?"

Paige glanced out the driver's side window as if she was avoiding Joey's gaze.

"Have you?" Joey repeated, already knowing the answer she was refusing to utter. "Well, clearly you fucking have," he tsked. "Have you banged him since?"

"We're not talking about this," Paige bristled. Her knuckles were turning white as they clenched the steering wheel.

"We don't have to. Your lack of response is response enough," he sighed, shaking his head in disapproval.

"Well aren't you judgmental!" she exclaimed, shooting daggers into Joey's eyes with her own. "You have no place judging anyone!"

"I didn't say anything," Joey replied, waving his hand dismissively in his sister's peripheral vision. "That was all you, judging yourself because you know damn well it's what your weak ass deserves."

Joey's body violently jerked forward as Paige slammed on the brakes and threw the car in park. Leaning over him to open the passenger door, Paige demanded, "Get out."

"You're crazy," he laughed, planting his butt in the seat.

"I'm serious." she stated, unlatching his seatbelt so she could push him out of the car.

Holding onto the door handle, Joey fought the trajectory. "Stop it, you psycho!"

"How weak am I now, huh?" she demanded. It was rare that Paige could assert her might over Joey, but the rage behind her final shove had him tumbling to the street.

"Oh c'mon," Joey chuckled, brushing his pants off. "You had to know I was gonna give you shit. When you do dumb fucking things, you get shit. That's, like, the rules of life."

He got back into the car without resistance.

"Should we talk about all the dumb fucking things you do?" Paige asked with her eyebrows raised to her hairline. "Because you do a lot of dumb shit."

"No doubt," he agreed, settling back into his seat. "I do a stupid amount of dumb shit. You could roast me on it for days."

"Years," Paige amended. "I don't have the energy. I used all of it getting you onto the street."

"That was savage."

"It could have been worse. I could've driven away."

"Honestly, you should have," Joey chuckled. "I would've been really, really pissed but that would've been such a badass move, man."

"There's still time," Paige warned, punching her fist against her palm.

"Keep your hands on the wheel, Thug Life," he teased. "You should handle that dickhead like you handle me. Maybe he'd give you some more respect."

Paige nodded sarcastically. "Yes, because domestic abuse is a great way to gain respect."

"It's only domestic abuse if you're living together. So technically, you domestically abuse me. He's fair game."

"Your moral compass is, like, perpetually broken."

"Says the girl who slammed on her brakes and pushed her little brother onto the street."

"My little brother," Paige laughed.

"You're arguing facts now?"

"You're wearing me out," she sighed. "You need to start smoking weed again. You're more annoying when you're not high."

Joey dropped his jaw in mock shock.

"They'll probably tell you you're expelled at the council meeting on Thursday anyway. It's not like you're getting tested tomorrow."

Paige had a point. Joey had been refraining from smoking in order to set a new normal, but he wouldn't know anything about school for several days.

"You're worse than Em and Mattie," Joey told her.

"Oh man, that's bad," Paige grinned. "Hey, did I tell you that Lilly despises Mattie?"

"No, but the feeling's mutual."

"I don't get it. What happened between them?" Paige wondered. "You can ask Lilly. Maybe she'll tell you."

"I can't get it up to care," Joey admitted.

After all, he had his own shit to worry about.

## 17

By the time the school board meeting rolled around, Joey was significantly less anxious than he had been earlier in the week. Though he had wanted to, he hadn't smoked weed, finding it somehow satisfying to deny his desire. He hadn't realized how much marijuana clouded his mind until it was forced to be less fuzzy. Joey had never considered himself a lackluster waiter. In fact, his capability to give people a good dining experience while simultaneously charming them was an attribute he took pride in. Still, his job had become markedly easier—and he believed he was more effective—thanks to his unclouded head. Prior to his waning weed habit, Joey had had a propensity to forget a table's requests. It wasn't out of the ordinary to receive a slew of reminders for soda refills or ramekins of ranch dressing. It was such a common occurrence that Joey was often jolted out of a sound slumber by the foreboding feeling that he was forgetting something. Despite his increased productivity, the nightmare still made its weekly appearance, leaving him to wonder if perhaps its meaning was less about his job and more about some other aspect of his life.

Joey didn't think much of his dreams, but he did find the fact that they existed fascinating in its own right. It was wild that he could close his eyes and end up in a different world, one that—depending on the night—was more terrifying or wonderful than reality. In dreams, he could get laid, something he found more challenging to accomplish when he was awake. The dream men were dominant and delicious in ways Joey doubted actual boys could be. Common stress dreams where he'd end up naked in front of a group of people didn't affect Joey in the way they bothered other people. It was liberating to be exposed, to be seen, especially when the eyes drinking him in were those of the men Missouri didn't house.

Though it was said that truth is stranger than fiction, for Joey, reality was odder than his dreams. Sitting at the school board meeting in an itchy blue sweater his mother bought for the occasion and insisted he wear, he wished he was anywhere but there. As much as he craved the gazes of others, the attention was daunting when it came from a faction of people who were tasked to make decisions about his life. The board didn't know him. The only information they had to help them come to their conclusion was what the scholastic reports provided and anecdotal input from teachers.

Bouncing his leg, Joey attempted to concentrate on the conversation going on at the table before him. Though the board members were discussing his future, it was painfully boring. He couldn't imagine living as unfulfilling a life as they did. Opining on the "mistakes" of students was probably the highlight of their week. Joey could never imagine caring about what other people did enough to give them ramifications for their actions.

"Stop," Bridget urged, placing her hand on Joey's knee to steady it. "On second thought, keep going. It's good they see you care."

His mother's whispers drew the attention of the board and a slew of sour faces.

"They're cheery," Paige muttered, squeezing Joey's other knee.

The show of support aggravated Joey. He wasn't as worried as his family wanted to believe he was. He would be fine either way. He always was. A few hours of anxiety had convinced them he was vulnerable. They should have known he was more empowered than that. Joey had spent fifteen years seeing rules as suggestions, and he wasn't about to kowtow to authority to gain something he wasn't moved by to begin with.

It reminded Joey of the odd cleaning kick his mother had gone on a few months before. She had read some book about getting rid of things that didn't make her happy. Bridget would put her hand on items in her closet and determine whether or not they brought her joy. Paige and Joey had had a field day making fun of her. They followed her around as she touched socks and asked herself aloud if they brought her joy. Joey wasn't sure how fucking socks brought anyone joy and figured his mother would end up sockless at the end of the experiment. It was crazy to think that the question had stuck with him after he mocked the process so extensively. Does this bring me joy? He wanted everything he touched in his life to make him happy even though he knew it was an impossibility. Things didn't work that way, but that didn't stop Joey from wishing they did. People surrendered their quest for complete joy too easily. He was impelled to reach for every shred of it. As far as he knew, he was only going to live one life. He wanted to make the most of it.

Suddenly grasping his mother's bicep in an action that clearly took Bridget completely by surprise, Joey whispered, "Does this bring me joy?"

"What?" she gasped, her eyes wide. "What are you talking about?"

"Does this bring me joy?" he repeated, earning a kick in the ankle from Paige.

"Shut up," she hissed, gesturing toward the condescending scowls from the peanut gallery.

"This shouldn't bring you joy," Bridget chided. "There's no joy in this."

"I meant you," Joey corrected, grinning at his mother. "And, congratulations, you do."

"I'm so relieved," Bridget huffed, shaking her head in annoyance.

As soon as Joey turned to Paige, the look on her face helped him to immediately determine that she didn't bring him joy, at least not at that moment. "You're a no."

"I'm brokenhearted," Paige said impassively. "I don't know how I'm going to deal with this information."

"You'll find a way," Joey promised, smiling at his sister as he looped his fingers around her wrist. "You're skinny."

Paige shook him off her. "Shh."

Joey sighed and sunk lower in his seat. No matter the outcome, he wanted the meeting over.

He was wasting away under the fluorescent lights of hypocrisy. There was no chance that the people sitting in the room hadn't messed around with drugs. And if by a slim chance they hadn't, they should have.

"We have one of our high school guidance counselors, Mr. Seaver, here to speak on Mr. Mills' behalf," the school board president announced, waving Mr. Seaver up to the desk in front of the board.

The counselor held eye contact with Joey as he took the seat. He had to give it to Seaver, the guy was good with follow-through. As far as Joey could tell, there was no reason for the older man to help him out. Joey had deceived him, and the test, for the past several months. He had to respect the fact that Seaver showed up to begin with, and it was even more impressive—if not confusing—that he was speaking to Joey's character.

"You may begin," the president directed.

"I've known Joey Mills for approximately three and half months. I inherited his case from his freshman year counselor, Mr. Capersen. I'll be honest with you, Joey's grades are abysmal, his attendance is even worse, and he failed his most recent drug test."

Bridget cringed and leaned over to ask Joey, "Didn't they say that he was speaking on your behalf? It doesn't sound like he's a big fan of yours, baby."

Joey clicked his tongue. "I have no idea what he's up to. Seaver's okay, but he's one of them."

"One of them? You sound paranoid," Paige admonished.

"And with all of that said, I still believe in the kid," Mr. Seaver admitted, looking over his shoulder at Joey, who was compelled to grin in return. "I don't know why, but I do. He has a fire in him, a charm that's not common in kids his age. I believe that with the proper guidance, he can do great things."

"Are you saying that as his counselor you haven't been giving him proper guidance?" one of the board members questioned, raising a bushy grey eyebrow incredulously.

"That was a burn," Paige whispered.

His interest reinvigorated, Joey continued to tune in to the conversation.

"There's only so much one can do in such a short period of time and under the circumstances," Mr. Seaver contended.

"That sounded like a dig at me," Bridget noted quietly.

"Shh," Joey hushed. "I can't hear."

"Oh, suddenly he's interested," Bridget told Paige, who shrugged in response.

"And what do you suggest as far as terms go?" the vice president of the board asked.

"How do you intend to keep him on the right path?"

"With all the patience I can muster," Mr. Seaver replied.

The statement had the board murmuring to one another and the president excusing Mr. Seaver and calling for a brief recess.

Five minutes turned to ten and then twenty as Joey awaited his fate. Mr. Seaver didn't stay in the room and avoided eye contact with Joey as he hustled out. It was odd, but Joey didn't have the mental energy to focus on anything but the decision.

When the board took their seats a half hour later, the Mills family sat up expectantly.

"Though it's unorthodox for us to give a student another chance after they have already had a drug infraction, the board was moved by Mr. Seaver's statements and will readmit Joey to Pacific High School with caution. Mr. Mills will take weekly drug tests and increase his attendance and grade point average to be that of which we expect from our student athletes. If by the end of the term Joey has not met these goals, we will reconvene on this matter and discuss next steps," the president explained. He turned his attention directly to Joey. "You got lucky, young man."

Joey let out the breath he hadn't realized he'd been holding. Though it felt like everything had changed, it all had remained the same. He would be back at Pacific High School on Monday morning, back in Seaver's office, and no doubt, back on his bullshit.

## 18

"I'm not gonna lie," Joey said, standing on the hearth of the fireplace with his arms raised above his head and a fifth of Jack Daniels in his hand, "this feels really fucking good."

"I thought you didn't care," Paige teased, flopping down on the couch beside Emily. "It seems like you care now."

"I love a victory, Paige," Joey replied, taking a swig directly from the bottle. "And this was a victory, even if the outcome is school."

"At least it's school with us," Mattie reasoned, kneeling in front of Joey. "Hit me."

Joey grinned at his friend and placed the bottle on her lips before tilting it forward to pour the amber alcohol down her throat. He stopped when she surrendered and smacked his shin.

Coughing and shuddering—presumably from the taste—Mattie wiped her mouth with the back of her hand. "Fuck."

"I wasn't going to give you a pussy pour," Joey tsked playfully. "C'mon, Mattie. You're better than that." He grinned at Paige and Emily. "Who's next?"

The deluge continued until the bottle was empty and the crew was adequately wasted. Since Bridget and Steve were working late, they didn't worry about the music's pounding bass or the shrieks of wild laughter that were filling the living room. Everything was new and exciting with Joey's second lease on his school career signed, sealed, and Seavered.

The whole ordeal had Joey exhilarated by a foreign yet somewhat familiar emotion. He'd had blips of invincibility in the past, but the sustained feeling that he was untouchable was more intoxicating than whiskey ever could be. There was no denying he was drunk on the power his personality afforded, but he wasn't delusional enough to overlook the implicit danger that came with riding that train of thought.

It wasn't a physical assurance in himself as much as an increased confidence in his capabilities to slip out of sticky situations and the belief that there was nothing that could bring him down. He hadn't given Mr. Seaver any reason to stand up for him, yet the counselor did. He'd caused his mother an obscene amount of stress, but she sat by his side at the school board meeting and every other disciplinary hearing—a constant source of support. Joey had lashed out at every person he loved, and besides his dad, they'd all stayed. It wasn't that he wanted to push people away, it was just that he did, and though he probably should have been, he was never left alone to wallow in misery or cope with the ramifications of his actions.

He was almost free of fear, which made the fact that he was so tentative about his sexuality even more frustrating. He wasn't a person who cared about what others thought of him. Joey was lighting in a bottle, unable to be contained by glass but easily extinguished by a storm inside. To be constrained was so unnatural, but it was all he'd known regarding the heat he felt for men.

Being gay was the only part of Joey that reminded him he wasn't invincible. He wasn't shamed by it but humbled. Though he had always found a way to cope with his life easily, his life had never been easy. He could blame his father or his parents' youth for the struggles, but it wasn't fair, and he knew it. He was quietly tormented by the compulsion to hide what didn't need to be hidden. The trepidation he felt was so out of the ordinary that it stalled him in a place he didn't want to stay. Yet he did.

"You're obliterated," Emily laughed as Joey gyrated his hips and climbed onto her lap. She turned to Paige. "Have you seen him do this shit? A few shots and he's a stripper."

"I haven't," Paige replied. "Which is a relief. I could live my whole life and be glad not to see it."

"But now you have," Joey grinned, leaning his head back as he continued to move to the music. "Drink it in, P."

"It sounds like you just said 'drink pee' but in Yoda's way," Mattie pointed out before doing her best impression of the Star Wars character. "Drink it in pee, if you will."

"Here I thought Joey was the only mess," Paige chuckled.

"You know who's a mess?" Mattie asked.

Joey knew the question wasn't rhetorical, though he wished it was. He couldn't listen to another rant about Lilly.

"Who?" Emily inquired, earning a glare from Joey. "What?"

"You're more drunk than you look," Joey admonished.

"Oh yeah? And you can tell that through these bleary eyes," Emily retorted, poking her fingers rhythmically against Joey's eyelids.

"Lilly," Mattie said. The statement surely wasn't a surprise to anyone in the room. "Joey told me she's selling synthetic weed now?"

"Yeah, it's awesome stuff, a K2 strain called Mad Hatter," Paige replied.

Joey could hear his sister's defensiveness, something Mattie seemed to be oblivious to.

"So, she's a drug dealer now? I didn't take her for a drug dealer. It's kind of next level, don't you think?" Mattie continued.

"I mean, technically she's not a drug dealer. Mad Hatter isn't classified as a drug in our student handbook so ..." Paige shrugged and reached for the empty bottle of Jack. "Fuck, we killed it."

"That just means we have to get more," Joey decided, standing up to end his impromptu lap dance. He didn't want to hear bullshit discussions on his night to celebrate. He needed everyone more drunk—like, to the level of incapacitation. If they were drunker, they'd be quieter, or louder but less coherent. He didn't want to think about anything other than his night and all the amazing nights to come. It was invigorating to pretend that the world worked on his whims and he would exploit the excitement for as long as he could.

"And how are we going to do that?" Mattie asked. "Do we know anyone that can buy us a bottle?"

"You know what's stupid?" Joey began, kneeling on the rug before deciding that he needed to be horizontal. Lying back on the ground, he watched as the ceiling fan moved through the same rotation indefinitely. The cool air gently lapped at his warm cheeks as he tried to remember what he was about to say.

"You?" Paige offered.

"What about me?" he asked, confused by his sister's random utterance.

"You're stupid," Paige asserted, shaking her head. "Honestly, it's not fun to give you crap when you're too wasted to fight back."

"I'm not wasted," Joey responded, but he certainly was.

"What's stupid?" Emily pressed, but in spite of the interest, he couldn't remember what he was going to say.

"Lilly?" Mattie suggested. "And her synthetic weed?"

"It definitely wasn't that," Joey stated. "That shit's genius. Lilly told me it gets you high as fuck and they can't detect it on drug tests."

"That's literally the last thing you need," Mattie huffed. "You're not thinking about getting into it are you?"

"I'm not thinking about anything," Joey replied. That wasn't a lie. Every thought that entered his mind quickly flitted away. He barely remembered the words he said a second after they were out of his mouth. And he loved it.

"He's not going to get into it," Paige told Mattie.

"You don't speak for me," Joey protested.

"So, you are?" Mattie questioned, standing over Joey.

He sighed. "I didn't say that."

"Yes you did," his friend argued.

Joey couldn't remember if he had or not, but he held his ground —from the ground. "Nope."

"He said Paige doesn't speak for him, but he didn't say he was going to smoke the stuff," Emily interjected.

"Thanks for your help," Mattie tsked, rolling her eyes.

"I hope you're giving her the finger," Joey called to Emily, "because she's giving you her stink eye."

"You're sloppy and selling me out," Mattie chuckled and nudged Joey's hip with her toes playfully. "I'm just looking out for you."

"Tonight should be proof that I'm good," Joey said, pushing his hair off his forehead as he smiled up at his friend. "I feel like a fucking mobster."

"A monster?" Paige repeated quizzically.

"Yeah, that too. Out there consuming the souls of boring school board members and living wild."

"Is there any other way to live?" Emily added.

Joey could hear the smile in her voice, so he smiled back, teeth beaming at the ceiling.

"I can text my friend Luke. He has a fake. He could probably get us some more Jack," Paige offered.

Knowing his sister as well as he did, Joey was aware that Paige was more over the conversation than he was.

Teetering to a sitting position, Joey pointed his finger at his confused sister. "Wait a minute."

"What?" she asked, barely glancing up from her phone.

"Is he the guy? This Luke guy, is he the one?"

"That's, like, the worst terminology to use in this situation," Paige huffed.

"You have a boyfriend?" Emily asked, surprised. "Are you talking about getting married or something?"

"What?" Paige cried. "No and fucking no! It's not like that at all."

"What was his name again? ... Luke," Joey said, proud of his brain for remembering an iota of something that mattered. "Fuck that guy. He should come here. He owes you that."

"Joey hates your boyfriend?" Mattie asked Paige, appearing to be just as confused as Emily.

"He never even mentioned you were with anyone."

"That's because I'm not," Paige sighed. "Why are we even talking about that?"

"She's not with him. He uses her whenever he wants to nut and then fucks off again," Joey explained.

The pillow slamming him in the face took him by surprise, and so did the subsequent stream of ice water that was poured over his head.

"Fuck you," Paige growled, disappearing from the room before Joey could reply.

"I guess we're not getting that bottle, huh?" he grumbled as he removed his saturated shirt and tossed it beside him. He looked from one shocked face to the other. "What?"

"You pissed her off majorly," Emily noted.

"Oh really? I didn't catch that," Joey snarked, knowing he had probably pushed his sister too far.

It was what it was. He wasn't wrong, and Paige would get over it. She always did. It was her fault for putting herself in that position. If she was embarrassed by the situation, she shouldn't have gotten herself into it to begin with. There were ramifications for actions. Or so he heard.

# 19

Paige ignored Joey for three days following the "Joey's Not Expelled" party for reasons he didn't entirely remember. Out of principle, he ignored her back, a tactic that no doubt infuriated his sister more. Mattie and Emily reminded Joey of what had gone down and told him he was in the wrong, which was fine. They could think whatever they wanted. Unlike Luke Whatever, Joey's heart was in the right place. He wasn't going to apologize for telling Paige what she needed to hear, even if it wasn't necessarily what she wanted to. What kind of brother would he be if he didn't tell her the hard truths about guys? If he didn't make her see it even when she wanted to keep her eyes closed? He never thought he had much of a protective instinct, but it seemed he did. Despite knowing that loyalty to his sister was a good thing, Joey found the desire to watch out for Paige to be daunting and uncomfortable. He didn't want to care about the ins and outs of anyone's life, even if they were family. Fuck, he didn't even want to give a shit about the details of his own.

"Paige!" Joey yelled from the bathroom. "Paige!"

The lack of response wasn't surprising, but his sister was the only person home and he desperately needed her help.

"Paige!" he screamed louder.

"What?" her aggravated voice called from the other side of the bathroom door.

"Get me toilet paper, please."

"You have to be fucking kidding me. Get it yourself," she growled.

"I'm serious. Stay mad at me; I don't care. Just give me a fucking roll."

He heard his sister stomp down the hallway to the linen closet, open the door, and then slam it shut. Joey expected her to pass him the paper, but instead he heard a soft thud.

"Where's that toilet paper?" he demanded, wondering what was taking her so long.

"Downstairs," she said simply. "Every roll in the house is downstairs." The sound of her bedroom door shutting made it clear to Joey that his sister wasn't in a helpful mood.

"Bitch," he grumbled, shimmying his jeans over his ankles so he could leave them on the bathroom floor.

Joey was nearly down the stairs when he heard a dramatic gasp and saw his stepsister Nicole standing in the kitchen, hand over her mouth as he stood in front of her in full glory. He was glad to have no shame because if he got embarrassed easily, the circumstance would've been mortifying.

"Paige threw all of the T.P. down here," he explained as he collected the rolls. "She's a savage."

"What did you do to her?" Nicole asked, placing her hands on her hips. "You had to do something to piss her off so royally."

Joey waved his free hand dismissively. "She's always angry about something."

Nicole raised a skeptical eyebrow and Joey smirked back. His stepsister knew him well. Nearly five years older than him, Steve's only biological child was wiser and more astute than Joey could contend with while standing in the middle of the kitchen naked.

"I heard you almost got expelled," Nicole noted, popping a grape into her mouth.

"Yeah, it was wild," Joey confirmed. "I thought I was a goner and then ..."—he paused for a beat—"I wasn't."

"Wild," she agreed.

Joey was about to head upstairs when Steve entered the kitchen with two coffees from Starbucks and an unimpressed expression on his face. "Well, this wasn't a sight I was expecting to see," Steve stated, "but somehow it's not shocking that you're standing in the middle of the kitchen with your dick out."

"Paige threw all the toilet paper down here," Joey stated.

"Ah, she's still angry with you," Steve nodded. "That makes sense."

"Did she tell you about it?"

"A bit," Steve answered.

"Oh, this is normal," Paige deadpanned, as she traipsed into the kitchen and grabbed a handful of grapes.

"Just a typical Sunday morning here, huh?" Nicole laughed, "You know, sometimes I regret not growing up in this circus."

"It's an adventure," Paige stated, narrowing her eyes at Joey. "Why are you naked?"

Struggling with the rolls so he could give his sister the finger, Joey grunted, "You know why I'm naked. And now you get the back view."

With that, he plodded up the stairs, giving the spectators a little wiggle as he did.

"Nasty ho!" Paige called after him. He heard her laugh, an act he was positive was despite herself.

"Stop talking about yourself like that," Joey remarked, glancing back for long enough to see Paige rolling her eyes in his wake. "I love you, P."

"Why don't you prove it by shutting the fuck up?" she suggested.

"You got it," Joey replied, giving his sister a cheesy smile before shaking his ass again. As he made his way to the bathroom, he grinned. He loved arguing with Paige. She was so fun to aggravate and he knew she felt the same about him.

Locking the door, Joey got into the shower, letting the hot water wash over his body. Though he tried not to let it get to him, the fact that he was headed back to school the next day had him feeling particularly introspective. What had been a victory a few days prior was now nothing more than a disappointment. He didn't want to go back to school. He wanted to focus his attention on enjoying his life, something that was impossible to do when he was wasting his time in a classroom. It was an exhausting prospect to know he was expected to rot at Pacific High School for the next three years—four if he counted the amount of credits he was behind. There had to be an end point, a moment when he came to terms with the very real chance that he'd never graduate. The realization didn't bother him, but he couldn't pretend indefinitely that it wasn't the case. His outlook on most things was unorthodox, but there were so few expectations that anyone put on him other than a diploma. His education, or lack thereof, was what would stand out to his mother as the sign that she had somehow failed. And it wouldn't be true, but it wouldn't matter, because society would think otherwise and Bridget would suffer. Though Joey didn't care what people thought of him, he didn't want to be a permanent mark on his mother's life. She'd struggled enough.

A banging on the wall jarred Joey from his rumination and prompted him to shut off the shower.

"You better leave some hot water for the rest of us," Paige yelled.

"Why are you so obsessed with me this morning?" Joey groaned, turning the water back on.

The knocking persisted as he took his time and then some. When the distraction finally subsided, Joey climbed out of the shower and wrapped a towel around his waist. A light rap on the door requested Joey to open it, so he did.

"I don't want to fight anymore," Paige stated, shutting the toilet seat to sit on it.

"Yes you do. You love it," he accused. "It gives you energy like it does me."

"We've always been fighters," she agreed, "but it's better when we're not fighting each other."

"Did you have this realization while you were throwing the toilet paper downstairs?"

"Kind of," Paige grinned. "And when you twerked your way up the steps."

"That wasn't twerking. I can show you twerking if you want."

"I saw your dancing the other night. We're good," Paige replied, holding her hands up in resistance. "Anyway, I accept your apology."

"I didn't apologize," Joey reminded her.

"Oh. Well, then go ahead."

"What am I apologizing for?"

"Really?" Paige tsked. "You embarrassed me in front of your friends and you don't even remember doing it?"

"I vaguely remember," Joey said as he squeezed toothpaste onto his toothbrush. "Why do you care what they think about you? They're nothing to you."

Paige cringed. "That's extreme. How much do people have to mean to me to give a shit what their perceptions are?"

"If you were me, a whole hell of a lot," Joey admitted. "I literally care what two people think."

"Which two?" Paige questioned with a smirk.

"It changes with the day."

"Like your moods."

"Mm-hmm," Joey hummed. He wanted to assert that she was more moody than him, but he didn't want to hear her talk for another twenty minutes. "I'm a moody one."

"Finally, you admit it," Paige chuckled. "Anyway, what I'm about to tell you isn't me co-signing any of the asshattery or giving my consent for what you're getting yourself into …"

"Now I'm interested," Joey remarked, turning to give Paige his full attention. "And I've never asked for anyone's consent to do anything."

"We're all painfully aware."

"What is it?" Joey pressed.

"Lilly said you're interested in buying some of her synthetic shit, so she's going to give you a good deal. I texted you her number and she's open to hearing from you if you're down," Paige said.

"Oh, I'm so down."

"I figured you would be."

"Do you think she can get me something for tomorrow?" Joey asked. His return to school wouldn't be a dud if he had some undetectable mind-alterer moving through his system.

"You can't get fucked up before school, you idiot! Especially not on your first day back," Paige admonished. "Suddenly, I regret telling Lil I'd give you her number."

"Regret is such a shitty emotion," Joey sighed. "You should try to feel less of it."

Paige raked her fingers through her hair and shook her head. "You're a lunatic, do you know that?"

"I've heard," Joey replied easily, his mouth frothing with minty toothpaste. "Believe it or not, you're not the first person to say it."

"I believe it, wholeheartedly."

Spitting into the sink, Joey gave his sister a still-sudsy smile. "Me too. There are worse things to be."

"Oh yeah? Like what?" Paige indulged.

"Boring. That's a horrible thing to be. So many people are so boring."

"Do you think I'm boring?"

"It's impossible for you to be boring," Joey promised, wiping his mouth with the hand towel lying on the counter. "I'm your brother."

Paige sighed and mirrored Joey's grin. "That's what it is?"

"I keep things interesting."

"I can't deny that, but I can keep it interesting too."

"Bet." Joey nodded before taking Paige's hand to yank her up into a hug. "Don't forget what a feisty one you are."

Paige didn't reply, and Joey was worried that his sister already had.

## 20

Though he hated to agree with Paige, Joey decided that getting high on his first day back wasn't a great idea. He didn't mind trouble, but there was a difference between dealing with it and knowingly inviting it in for little to no reason. He felt stable and reasonable—two attributes he rarely possessed, and qualities he found completely overrated. School was boring to begin with, but without a buzz, it was unbearable. Evidently, his first period teacher had given up on attempting to be engaging. He didn't understand why it was so challenging for teachers. It wasn't difficult to be interesting. He kept his classmates hanging on every word. Granted, his subject matter was a lot more scandalous than what his teachers taught, but he was sure he could make the Civil War fascinating too. It was about storytelling. Joey's confidence in his orating ended at Algebra though—that shit was a lost cause.

The almost-expulsion had caused a spike in his popularity. People loved a badass, and his rap sheet had confirmed he was just that.

"My man," a senior Joey didn't recognize greeted, shaking Joey's hand as he walked past him in the hallway.

"What's up?" Joey responded, grinning at the guy and the two hot football players he was with.

If that was the type of attention he could pull from escaping expulsion, Joey wasn't opposed to capitalizing on it. He licked his lips, trying to push visions of a locker room gang bang from his mind. "Hello" shouldn't have so easily spurred a hard-on. He needed to get laid, preferably by a well-endowed wide receiver. It was getting to the point that he would settle for a water boy as long as he was good looking and down to do it. The more time he spent thinking about fucking and not fucking doing it, the bigger deal the whole concept of sex became. And more intimidating.

It was crazy that he could attend a board meeting where strangers discussed the fate of his scholastic life and remain mostly unfazed, yet the thought of being intimate with another boy was anxiety-inducing. He needed to use a hookup app and get over it. That was the only way to make it a nonissue and relieve his apprehension. It wasn't a big deal. He just had to do it to prove that to himself. Adjusting the straining in his briefs as he continued toward English class, Joey resolved to create a profile and get on with it.

"Look at you all bright-eyed and bushy-tailed," Emily exclaimed as Joey slid into the desk next to her. "How does it feel?"

"How does what feel? Being back in school?"

Emily smirked. "Being in English class. How long has it been?"

"Not long enough," Joey stated, glancing at the inspirational posters hanging on the walls.

"Do you think they believe that shit?"

"Who believes what shit?"

"Teachers. Do you think they believe the bullshit on the posters they have all over their classrooms?" he wondered. "Like, 'There's no such thing as a stupid question.' Do you think they really believe that? That there's no such thing a stupid question?"

"Maybe," Emily shrugged. "Some of them are probably delusional enough to believe it. I mean, some teachers actually wear Christmas sweaters without trying to be ironic, so ..."

Joey nodded. "Valid point."

As his hand shot up in the air, Emily's eyes grew wide. "What are you doing?"

"Seeing if Ms. Green agrees that there aren't any stupid questions," Joey replied with a cheeky grin.

"You're an idiot."

"I'm perpetually bored," Joey disagreed. "If I were an idiot, I wouldn't worry about any of this stuff. I would just sit here like a lump, being useless."

"What's up, Joey?" Ms. Green asked. She appeared to be aggravated by his mere existence, a variable that would most likely skew his experiment.

"Do you really think there's no such thing as a stupid question?" he wondered.

"In what regard?" the teacher asked, pushing the cap onto the white board marker in her hand.

Joey wordlessly pointed at the poster.

"Oh. I'd say it depends on the intention of the querent. Any pursuit of knowledge can't be considered stupid," Ms. Green replied in a manner that was more thoughtful than he expected. "If the aim of the person asking the question is to provoke, they may purposely ask something solid to aggravate another person, and in that case, I would concede that there was in fact such a thing as a stupid question."

Rendered speechless by the response, Joey smiled at Ms. Green before quickly shutting his mouth. He could see why so many guys in his class had a crush on their teacher. She was young, pretty, and smart in a way that wasn't intimidating as much as it was inspiring. It was easy to deduce that Ms. Green had never faced expulsion for a drug offense or set a trailer on fire, but she was a badass in her own right. There was something to be said for gaining that type of credibility on the merit and sting of one's words alone. He liked it. He liked her.

When the bell signaled the end of class, Joey moved slowly, waiting for everyone else to leave the classroom before approaching his teacher.

"That was a good answer," he told Ms. Green as she straightened the papers on her desk.

She grinned at the compliment. "I'm glad you thought so."

"I was going to give you shit," Joey admitted, narrowing his eyes when Ms. Green laughed.

"I'm quite aware."

"And that doesn't bother you?" he questioned, beginning to gnaw on his fingernails. It wasn't a nervous habit as much as a creature comfort from his formative years that hadn't fully gone away.

"Childish antics don't bother me. If they did, I wouldn't be a teacher," she said with a wink of one of her blue eyes.

"Childish, huh?" Joey mused. The statement would have bothered him if it had come from another teacher, but the mischievous look on Ms. Green's face was so relatable that he wasn't bothered.

"Mm-hmm," she nodded. "Grown people don't poke and prod for negative attention."

"I know plenty of adults who do."

"You don't have to be a child to be childish, and you can be an adult without being grown. It's all about maturity." Ms. Green stopped shifting the papers on her desk to give Joey her full attention. "You value power, don't you?"

Joey was skeptical, but intrigued. "How do you figure?"

"Well, it's obvious by how infrequently you actually show up to school that you seek a high level of autonomy. I don't believe it's solely because you're disinterested in learning; I think it's due to your desire to control all aspects of your life, a feat that's nearly impossible at fifteen years old. But you're still going for it, which is as admirable as it is misguided." Ms. Green took a sip of her coffee. It may as well have been tea. "People think power is the ability to do as one pleases and push people around, but that's not it at all."

Joey had attended Ms Green's class sporadically over the past few months, so it was odd that the woman was reading him like one of the books on her shelves. He wondered if he was transparent or if his teacher was just that in tune.

"Are you a psychic?"

Ms. Green laughed and placed a dainty hand on her chest. "Not even close."

"How did you—" Joey began, but he was interrupted by her answer.

"I pay attention. You know that power you crave? The best way to get it," she shook her head and corrected herself. "The *only* way to get it is to pay attention. Ideally, you'd pay attention in class. There's so much to learn from the writings of the past, but at the very least, pay attention to the people around you. People will do anything for you if they feel valued. Do you feel valued?"

"In general?"

"In general or specifically. How about in this moment? Do you feel valued right now?"

Joey answered tentatively, "Um, I guess so."

"And that's why you'll do your English homework tonight and show up to class tomorrow," Ms. Green said matter-of-factly. "It's as simple as that."

"Oh, is it?" Joey asked with a smirk. "This is all it's going to take to get me on track?"

She gave him a knowing grin. "That's entirely up to you."

"You should give Seaver a few pointers. He's been trying to do that for a while."

"So, you admit that I've made some headway, then?"

"Did I?" Joey questioned. He could tell that she knew that she did, and he was alright with his teacher claiming the victory. "I guess I did."

"We will have to see if it translates to an increased commitment to your studies. If I'm being honest, I think it could go either way," Ms. Green admitted.

"Well, honestly, I think you're probably right," Joey agreed, pushing his hair back and grasping it between his fingers for a moment before letting go.

"What stands in your way?" she questioned, smiling at the students who were coming in to take their seats.

"I bet you're angling for me to say myself—that I'm what stands in my way."

"You're a smart kid, Joey Mills," Ms. Green replied, "and right now, you're a smart kid who's going to be late for third hour."

Joey nodded and headed out of the room. He didn't make a habit of talking to teachers, but if he did, Ms. Green would be one he wouldn't mind spending more time with. It was rare that he was compelled to listen to the advice of others, but much of what Ms. Green said resonated with him.

And he liked that enough to look forward to second period the next day.

As he walked toward third period, Joey debated whether he should actually go to Algebra II or if he should cut and work on his dating profile. Dating. It was a funny concept. He wasn't sure why his mind immediately jumped to the "romantic" component. Maybe it was an odd form of rationalization. He wasn't going to date. Did people his age really date? What was the purpose anyway? Dating was basically an interview process for marriage and he wasn't about to get locked down at fifteen, or really at any age at all.

Suddenly, Algebra seemed more appealing than a dating app. Fucking could wait. Even Ms. Green knew that he liked his freedom.

## 21

Most of the responsibility Joey had exhibited on Monday had gone by the wayside by Tuesday. The fact that he intended to attend school for two days in a row was accomplishment enough. Though he wasn't particularly interested in turning over a new leaf, it wasn't worth cutting off his nose to spite his face for a few extra hours in bed. There were a lot of eyes on him, and he didn't want to give them anything to look at—at least not for a while. Joey did, however, want to see everything less clearly. Monday had been crisp and focused, and he needed Tuesday to be fuzzy and faded. That was why he decided to go up to the track and smoke some of Lilly's K2 instead of going to first period.

*Emily (7:56am): Did one day burn you out, Burnout?*

*Mattie (7:56am): I'm guessing that question is meant for Joey.*

*Emily (7:57am): Good guess considering I saw you in the hallway ten minutes ago. Did you see him?*

*Mattie (7:57am): Nope*

*Emily (7:57am): Hear from him?*

*Mattie (7:57am): Also a no.*

*Emily (7:58am): Do you think he would actually skip?*

*Mattie (7:58am): Is that a serious question? Of course he would!*

Joey watched as the messages appeared on the screen, wondering how long they would discuss his assumed absence. As much as he appreciated having friends who cared about him, he never liked being under a microscope. Sometimes he wanted to fall off the face of the Earth and float in a galaxy of his own—free from expectations. He loved Emily and Mattie, but they didn't wholly understand him, nobody did. How could anyone truly know another person if they didn't live under their skin, feel their blood pumping through their veins, know the rhythmic pattern of their heart? It was easy to feel alone when he realized that he was the only person who would ever be able to call his body a home.

*Emily (7:59am): I'm going to kill him. It's not that difficult NOT to fuck up.*

*Mattie (8:00am): But he doesn't think he's fucking up. That's literally not even a consideration for him.*

*Emily (8:00am): How could it not be? Joey, how could it not be?*

*Mattie (8:01am): He's probably sleeping. Don't cyber bully him.*

*Emily (8:01am): Questioning his shitty choices isn't cyber bullying.*

*Mattie (8:02am): Whatever. On to the important shit.*

*Emily (8:02am): Like what?*

*Mattie (8:02am): You'll see.*

*Emily (8:03am): You can't do that! You can't change the subject and then get shady as fuck. It's illegal.*

*Mattie (8:03am): Do you know what else is illegal? Dealing.*

*Emily (8:04am): Well, lucky for us, we're not drug dealers.*

*Mattie (8:04am): Even luckier today and that's all I'm going to say, or type—whatever!*

*Emily (8:05am): Whatever.*

*Mattie (8:05am): Whatever.*

*Emily (8:05am): Whatever!*

*Mattie (8:05am): WHATEVER!!*

Unable to stop himself from jumping in on the annoying conversation, Joey started typing:

*Joey (8:06am): Wow. You guys are intense in the morning.*

*Mattie (8:06am): Why should the morning be any different from the rest of the day?*

*Emily (8:07am): Where are you?*

*Joey (8:07am): Chilling. I'll be there by second period.*

*Emily (8:08am): Somebody wants to see Ms. Green!*

*Mattie (8:08am): Oh man. Do we need to add you to the list of dudes who wanna fuck her?*

Joey didn't want to tell his friends that he was smoking the synthetic. In the past, he would have included them in the act, but Mattie's vendetta against Lilly meant she would give him an epic amount of shit for buying it from her. He definitely wasn't in the mood to deal with her emotions when he was busy avoiding his own.

*Joey (8:09am): Lame.*

*Emily (8:09am): Yes you are! You were hanging on her every word yesterday.*

*Joey (8:09am): She's the teacher. Who else am I supposed to be listening to?*

*Mattie (8:10am): Name another teacher you focus on…we'll wait.*

*Joey (8:10am): Keep waiting.*

He had twenty minutes to kill before class and he wasn't going to spend it on bullshit. So what if he was interested in hearing what a teacher had to say? It was a strange position to be in to have people expect him to be such a fuckup that anytime he did something moderately "typical" it was questioned.

Lying on the cold, packed dirt of the track, Joey admired the ombré grey clouds. From slate to white, they looked like the waves of an angry ocean, stirred by the wind and capped with snow. They were majestic and foreboding, a combination that left him in awe of their immensity and his insignificance. Perhaps that was why he liked to get high, because the world was more impressive when he left the ground.

Life on land was weird. No matter how much his friends and family loved him, they didn't really know him. How could they? They only saw what he let them see, and he didn't show them a big part of himself. Mattie and Emily thought he wanted to fuck Ms. Green. It was crazy that they actually believed he would want to be with a woman. Though he wasn't outward with his attraction to men, the fact that he never talked about girls should have been some sort of indicator. Maybe they were aware and were just waiting for him to come out, maybe he should have already, maybe he would sometime. It was a daunting consideration. And one he didn't want to think about extensively. He hated how much weight it held when he was focused on the light.

As the sun seeped through the slivers of space in the stratified cloudscape, Joey took another hit from his pipe, letting the Mad Hatter muddy his mind. Having set an alarm to remind him when it was time to go to Ms. Green's class, Joey concentrated on the deep inhales that burned his lungs and the chilly air cooling his face. Though he enjoyed being around people, he loved moments like those, when time stopped for just long enough to settle into it. He wasn't bored, lonely, or worried. He was satisfied and that was awesome.

The phone vibrating in his pocket interrupted his reverie and he sighed as he pulled it out to see another message from Emily. It was unusual for her to text him separately from the group chat and it had him wondering what warranted the privacy.

*Emily (8:29am): Are you really planning to show up today?*
*Joey (8:30am): Yeah, I'll be there at the beginning of 2nd. What's up?*
*Emily (8:30am): Mattie's in Principal Lloyd's office.*
*Joey (8:31am): Shit, what did she do?*
*Emily (8:31am): I have no idea. I thought you might know. They called her out of class and she didn't seem surprised.*
*Joey (8:31am): Weird.*
*Emily (8:31am): Super weird.*
*Emily (8:31am): We'll have to grill her during lunch.*
*Joey (8:32am): I'm sure we won't have to push too much.*
*Emily (8:32am): Probably not. See you soon.*
*Joey (8:32am): Yup.*

It was out of the ordinary for Mattie to get in trouble. Unlike Joey, she stayed off administrators' radars. She wasn't a saint but kept a low profile, showed up to school, and did her work. He couldn't imagine what she could have done to end up in front of the principal. He was curious though.

*Joey (8:32am): U there?*
*Joey (8:32am): Bitch...*
*Joey (8:33am): Em said you got called to Lloyd's office.*
*Joey (8:33am): What did U do?*

The lack of response was disconcerting. Mattie was never more than a minute away from her phone, even when she was in class. She was still in the office, and it was weird as hell.

Taking one last drag of the Mad Hatter, Joey rose to his feet. He was surprised by how weak his legs were. The longer he stood, the more wobbly they became. Placing his pipe and stash into a plastic bag, Joey made his way to the bleachers to tuck the contraband under one of the slats.

With a spinning head and woozy stomach, Joey attempted to find his balance. The K2 had hit him harder than he was expecting. Suddenly, he regretted smoking the shit for the first time when he had to go to class afterward. When he heard the bell ringing in the school building several yards away, Joey began a walk through molasses in an effort to make it to English.

Joey's heart pounded with every heavy step he took as he trudged down the crowded hallway. He knew he wasn't functioning normally—a realization that became more terrifying as the fluorescents on the ceiling flickered, shutting off for several seconds at a time and flashing with the brightness of thousands of bulbs. He was fucked up, more fucked up than he ever remembered being. He needed to keep it together for long enough to get into his desk and put his head down. The nausea churning in his stomach had Joey doubting that the task was possible. He was going to pass out. There was no avoiding it. He was going to go down.

With a vague recognition that he had miraculously remained vertical, Joey kept pushing forward. He would get there. He had to get there.

"You're here," Ms. Green noted, her voice floating around his head like a halo. She continued to speak, but he couldn't discern the words. Her sentences were eerie melodies and his replies low devilish groans.

He didn't know what he was saying, but he hoped it was coherent. Noises from his mouth gave way to the rapid pulse of a metronome building tempo in his ears. With winter-kissed cheeks burning hot and cool beads of sweat gathering on his hairline, Joey tried to draw in a deep breath, realizing there was no air to be had. Terrified, he gasped again. The gasp echoed around him—the sick sound of suffering surrounding his exhausted body.

And then he was gone.

## 22

Joey had done a plethora of stupid shit in his life, but somehow he had never awakened in a hospital as a result of any of it. That was until he met his nemesis—the Mad Hatter. Whatever was in that synthetic weed had completely fucked him up and landed him in bed, hooked to numerous IV bags and draped in a paper-thin gown. Unfortunately, he wasn't alone. He could smell his mother's shampoo before he opened his eyes, and her presence inspired him to stay "asleep" for an hour longer than his body was compelled to.

Bridget was going to be pissed and Joey didn't blame her. He had taken it to a new level of irresponsibility. As much as he valued his independence, he didn't want to alienate his mother to the degree he knew he had. Scared people lashed out, tuned out. He couldn't afford for her to do either, not when he was in a hospital bed, not ever.

Joey's body was exhausted, but his brain was alive and not-so-well, plagued by terrifying thoughts of death. Maybe he was already dead. Maybe that was the joke of it all, that he was reflecting while nothing mattered anymore because he was already gone. His mother wasn't crying. She would cry if he was dead—he was sure of that, and he didn't hear any sniffles.

His frenzied heart rate had given way to a rhythmic beep on a monitoring machine. It was cold, sterile, and everything he never thought his heart could be, but it assured him he was alive, something he never thought he would wonder about. He'd always figured that death was the end, afterlife was a myth, and there was no consciousness in a rested soul, but what if he was wrong? What if death was an extension of life where he would exist in a parallel universe? It was an alarming prospect but not as terrifying as the chance that Heaven and Hell were real. He had always believed that the Christian view of afterlife was manufactured by the Church as a way to keep followers in line. The fear of Hell could steer people to make good choices, and the promise of Heaven rewarded their good behavior. It was appealing if one was free from sin, but Joey's desire to be free was a conduit for sin—and he rarely regretted it. There was no question in his mind that he was a good person, but that wouldn't stop him from going to Hell if it was real. Maybe every human was built to burn.

"He's awake," Steve said.

The deep voice breaking through the silence had Joey's body jerking in reaction.

"How can you tell?" Bridget asked.

"His eyelids are flickering. He's probably just too exhausted to open them. I think he can hear us though," Steve reasoned. "Joey, can you hear me?" He grew louder as Joey assumed he leaned in closer. "Joey."

"Quit it," Bridget chided. "If he could hear us, he'd respond."

"I doubt that, he's probably shitting himself."

Joey opened his eyes wide. Had he shit himself? He hadn't shit himself. "I'm not shitting," Joey grunted.

"I was speaking metaphorically, but I'm glad it inspired you to join us," Steve sighed. "What the fuck were you thinking, kid?"

Joey could have said that he wasn't thinking or some similar phrase that was proven to get parents off their kids' backs, but he decided to be honest instead. "That I wanted to get high. I don't know if it was laced with something or …"

"Or it could be because you smoked ..."—Bridget paused for long enough to take her phone out of her handbag and look the screen—"K2 Mad Hatter."

"Hmm?" Joey hummed. "Who told you that?"

"Principal Lloyd was alerted this morning that a Pacific High student was dealing the drug to a bunch of kids at school. You just happen to be the idiot who got messed up before school," she explained, shaking her head. "I don't know why you always get yourself into these situations."

Joey wanted to ask her if they'd tested his system to determine if it was K2 or if they assumed it was because of the narc, but he decided it wasn't worth it. He was fucked anyway. There was no coming back from another drug incident, especially less than a week after the board meeting.

"I'm tired," Joey muttered, closing his eyes. He didn't want to talk, and he figured that the needles in his arm had earned him at least a few hours of quiet.

Bridget and Steve didn't protest as they typically would, whispering to one another while Joey tried to tune them out. Despite the aggravation that had been on his mother's face, Joey knew she was worried, and though he wouldn't admit it, he was too. He'd been obliterated before, but he had never lacked complete control of his body. Passing out was scary as hell.

An immense pressure on his skull had Joey lifting his hand to rub his head. He needed something for the pain.

"You have a concussion," Bridget informed him.

"Can they give me morphine or something?" Joey questioned. "It's fucking throbbing."

"I doubt they make a habit of giving morphine to people who come in here for overdoses," Steve replied.

"I overdosed?" Joey cried, cringing when a dagger drove through the middle of his forehead as soon as he raised his voice.

"No, no," Bridget said, shaking her head vehemently and pointing her finger in Steve's face. "Stop. He didn't overdose. They said it was a negative reaction to the drug, not an overdose."

Steve nodded. "Not an overdose, but I doubt they're going to give you anything more than a Tylenol."

Joey groaned and stretched his legs out as far as he could while being contained in the hospital bed. He was about to close his eyes again when a crazy thought compelled him to sit up abruptly. "Where's my phone?"

Clearly frazzled by Joey's shift in energy, Bridget jumped at the request, clutching her chest as she did. "What?"

"My phone," he demanded frantically. "Where's my phone?"

"It's probably with your clothes," Bridget replied, rushing to the window seat to look.

She handed the phone over as soon as she found it, and Joey immediately scrolled through the messages on his home screen.

*Mattie (8:35am): I got Lilly.*

"Fuck," Joey groaned, trying to keep his hands steady as he read the rest of the texts.

*Mattie (8:36am): That stuff she's selling is poison anyway. It fucks people up majorly.*

*Emily (8:36am): Wait a minute, what do you mean you got her? Is that what you were doing in Lloyd's office.*

*Mattie (8:37am): Yup.*

*Emily (8:37am): Mattie!!*

*Mattie (8:37am): What? She was dealing an awful drug to a bunch of people. She deserves it.*

*Emily (8:38am): You didn't consider mentioning this to us before you did it? We usually talk this sorta stuff out.*

*Mattie (8:38am): What was there to talk about? She's wrong and I did the right thing. It is what it is.*

*Emily (8:39am): That's not our code.*

*Mattie (8:39am): What are we, a fucking gang? You're being really goddamn intense Em.*

"What's going on?" Bridget questioned, her tone rife with concern. "What are you upset about?"

Joey didn't answer. He was overwhelmed by the influx of information he had received. Toggling to the messages Mattie sent him separately from the group chat, Joey read them with a clenched jaw.

*Mattie (8:39am): I know you'd never narc anyone out, but you love a good revenge plot.*

*Mattie (8:39am): Don't pretend you don't.*

*Mattie (8:40am): I know she's Paige's friend but that girl is insufferable, Joey.*

*Mattie (8:40am): I literally hate you.*

*Mattie (8:40am): Stop ignoring me.*

*Mattie (8:42am): Asshole.*

*Mattie (8:49am): Omg. Wtf! Emily just texted me that you passed out in class. Are you ok?*

*Mattie (8:52am): I'm freaking the fuck out. Somebody said there's an ambulance in front of the school. You better be in the nurse's office and not on your way to the fucking hospital.*

*Mattie (9:01am): Text me as soon as you can. I'm losing it.*

*Mattie (9:16am): I know you're in the hospital but you better call me ASAP.*

*Mattie (9:47am): Seriously, I'm losing my mind over here.*

*Mattie (10:35am): I can't believe this. I'm so scared.*

If it wasn't for Mattie, the school officials might have thought he was having a seizure or something. They would have never known to test for a drug as random as K2, and the rest of his panel would have come back clean. Mattie's desire to fuck Lilly over had fucked Joey harder than she could have ever expected. He could barely fathom what the outcome would be for the trouble he found himself in.

"Are you going to tell us what's going on, or are we going to have to worry about this too?" Bridget inquired, pulling her blonde locks into a messy bun.

"Mattie was the person who told Principal Lloyd about the K2 on campus," Joey uttered, lying back on the bed as he attempted to digest the words he'd just said.

"No shit," Bridget gasped. "Really?"

Joey sighed, too confused about his emotions regarding the circumstances to formulate a coherent response.

"Did she know you were involved?" Steve asked. "I find it hard to believe she did."

Regardless of how angry his parents were, they knew and lived by the code Emily had referenced in her text. They minded their business and worried about their own. Thanks to Mattie's disregard of the simple rules of St. Louis, Joey was in a world of shit, an offense he didn't deem forgivable.

Joey wasn't obtuse. He knew that he'd invited the trouble into his life entirely on his own, but his propensity for fucking up was so strong that he didn't need any help ruining things.

The only help he needed was the type that would get him to the bathroom. He was lightheaded as hell.

## 23

Coming to terms with what Mattie had done wasn't going to happen while Joey was lying in a hospital bed. It was too much to think about when he was already physically and mentally exhausted by the day's events. As if that wasn't bad enough, the doctor had admitted him for overnight observation. He was glad that his mom and Steve had insisted on spending the night. The hushed whispers of nurses in the hallway, soft whir of medical machinery, and nauseating smell of bleach were unnerving.

Though Joey was independent as a child, he could vividly remember how often he turned to his mother for comfort. She used to call him her "cuddlebug" and he loved it. He would position himself on her body anytime she was horizontal, resting his head on her chest as she rubbed his back with one hand and played with his hair with the other. No matter what kind of trouble Joey had gotten himself into that day, Bridget never turned him away from a snuggle.

Opening his sleepy eyes, Joey glanced to his side. His mom was twisted in a pretzel-like position on the loudly upholstered chair in the corner. Her head was rested on Steve's shoulder as he sat stoically on a metal folding chair a nurse had brought in for him hours before.

"What's up?" Bridget whispered, arching her back and sighing when it cracked.

"Nothing," Joey replied, pursing his lips. He considered asking for what he needed, but decided against it. Instead, he turned to look at the mural of two hippopotamuses riding unicycles that was painted on the opposite wall.

When Joey realized earlier in the day that he was in St. Louis Children's Hospital, he was peeved. He was aware that he was a minor, but he certainly wasn't a kid. Supposedly, the EMTs had determined he wasn't going to die before he made it to the city center and protocol stated that they bring anyone under the age of eighteen to SLCH if they were capable of surviving the trip.

He didn't embarrass easily, but the fact that he was a teenager holed up in a baby hospital for getting too fucked up on a synthetic strain called "Mad Hatter" was objectively mortifying. It wasn't lost on him that doctors were taking time away from working with sick kids to concern themselves with K2. He wasn't selfish enough not to recognize how ludicrous the whole situation was. He was angry at his body for reacting to fake weed that way and at his brain or heart for reverting to childhood and craving care.

It was as if Bridget had read his mind. While he was focused on the painting, Joey felt thin fingers rake through his hair as his mother climbed into the bed beside him. Too proud to say a word, Joey kept his lips locked, relishing in the touch. Curling his head into his mother's body, Joey accepted the love he wasn't sure he deserved. He didn't know why he was driven to make everything complicated when it could be so simple. He wanted to be worthy of his mother's affection while living a life absent of consequence. Most people would say it wasn't possible, but Bridget consistently proved them wrong. She was a soldier, committed to her cause. Joey just hated how hard he made it all. His actions were never in retribution, but they weren't in respect either. He could have been better than he was if he wanted to be. He didn't understand why he didn't care enough to change.

A crying baby in the room next to him made it difficult for Joey to settle into the touch. The screaming was a reminder that he was in a place of pain—both experienced and caused. He didn't want any of it, yet there was no escaping, at least not for several more hours of observation.

"Somebody's unhappy," Steve noted, pulling one of the thin blue blankets up around his neck.

"It's weird that babies are in here," Joey stated. "What do you think's wrong with it?"

"It could be a lot of things," Bridget replied as she continued to tenderly massage Joey's head. "Babies aren't immune to all the things that older people go through."

"Like cancer and stuff?" Joey asked, surprised. It was unfathomable that a person who had barely been alive could face death.

"Yup. It's devastating to even consider," Bridget said, clipping her statement, visibly displaying her difficulty coping with the idea of it. "Horrible things happen every day. That's why you have to stop this shit, Joey. You don't want to invite the bad; it'll try to get in anyway. Don't make it easier."

Joey hummed his understanding and tilted his head toward his mother to give her easier access. Drifting in and out of sleep, he relished in the pacification. That was until the loud wailing of a woman rattled him from his rest. The anguish barely sounded human, growing more animalistic by the moment.

"What's that?" Joey uttered, feeling his pulse quicken as the screaming persisted.

A stampede of feet pounded against the tile floor as a man yelled "push epi!" "Again," he demanded. "Now!"

People continued to run into the room next door as Joey, Bridget, and Steve stared at one another, frozen with fear. Listening to the goings-on, Joey held his breath. It was the baby. It had to be the baby. They were in a children's hospital, how could it not be?

The mother's sobs echoed through the hall, haunting and full of despair.

"Someone get her out of here!" the man—who Joey deduced to be the doctor—ordered. "We need some space. C'mon!"

"Holy shit," Bridget croaked, her waterlines filling with tears as the whites surrounding her deep blue irises tinged red. "Close the door, Steve."

As his stepfather stood up to follow the directive, Joey said, "Don't."

It was the most horrible thing he'd ever seen—the mother curled in the fetal position on the floor as her husband held her crumpled body—but he couldn't stop staring. Joey had never witnessed a person break in front of him, had never seen a body give way to emotion in a way that left the vessel incapacitated. It was the personification of pain and it was devastating.

"I can't," Bridget cried, turning her head away. "Steve! He doesn't need to see this."

"Okay, okay," Steve confirmed, rushing toward the door. He closed it gingerly, rolling his lips in tight to contain the sadness Joey could see on his face.

Though Joey had protested when his mother had told Steve to do so before, he didn't try to stop the act for a second time. His mother was right. None of them needed to see what was happening. It was agonizingly intimate to watch someone as their world imploded.

Hearing it was bad enough.

Unfortunately, the walls were insubstantial, allowing the words, "Time of death: 10:41pm," to carry through.

"No! No, no, no," the mother sobbed in the hallway. Her howls vacillated between the repetition of "no" and moans of "my baby."

"Oh my lord," Bridget mumbled, shaking her head and burying her face in her hands.

"Wait," Joey began, his stomach growing sick at the thought. "The baby died? That's it? He's dead?"

Steve cleared his throat uncomfortably, "Um, it appears to be so."

"How old was he?" Joey fretted, sitting in the bed as his mom pulled herself up beside him. She tucked her hands under the opening in the back of his gown and dragged her fingertips across the span of his lats. "How old was that baby? He couldn't have been that old, right? He sounded really young when he was crying. Like, a really little baby." His eyes started to sting as the crushing sadness set in. "He was just a little baby!"

"Shh," Bridget shushed. "Shh, shh."

Bowing his head, Joey's tears slid down his hot cheeks and fell onto the scratchy white hospital blanket bunched on his lap. "Fuck," he groaned. Thoughts of the baby lying lifeless a few yards away were too much to bear. It wasn't fair. He hadn't lived even a fraction of his life and he was already dead. The baby was dead, and Joey was alive, actively making decisions that could lead to death without so much as a second thought.

He wondered what Bridget would do if she outlived him, if she were the woman inconsolable on the hospital floor. If she would spend the rest of her days dealing with the grief his death would bring her. Or if she would hold anger toward him and his memory for all the pain he had caused her, the way Joey did his father.

In the wake of the weeping mother and dead baby, Joey suddenly felt selfish. He had such little regard for his mortality, constantly challenging the bounds of survival for some fun. He didn't regret the way he lived, but he couldn't help but think of how his choices might affect his mother one day. He didn't know if what had happened with the K2 or in the hospital room next door to his would inspire him to make a long-term change in his behavior, but he did recognize that his decisions didn't solely impact him. It was something he knew before but hadn't understood in the way the situation had clarified.

Wiping his eyes and looking over his shoulder at Bridget's tear-stained face, Joey searched for words that would comfort each of them. Despite his loquacious nature, he couldn't think of any. Silently, he wrapped his arms around his mom's shoulders and held her as they both cried for the mother, her baby, and themselves.

## 24

Though he was in the hospital for less than twenty-four hours, the stay had profoundly impacted Joey. How could it not when lives had changed forever right in front of his eyes? In the past, he'd had the ability to push unsavory thoughts to the back of his mind or purge them completely to move forward. In spite of the skill set, Joey found it impossible to wash the woman's wails from his memory bank. Everything was darker than it had been days before. He had never considered himself innocent, though he was sure there had been a time when he was. The amount of trouble he got into immediately disqualified him from saint status. Fuck, he was facing a possible arrest for the Mad Hatter incident. Still, issues with school or the law didn't automatically equate to a loss of innocence. He wasn't dumb. The questionable decisions he made probably had a bit to do with naivety and more to do with his misfiring fear flares. Regardless of his choices, he'd never felt like he was in a different place than his age. He heard "mature" kids tout that they were "old souls," but he didn't know why they were proud of the distinction. He couldn't think of anything worse than having an "old soul." Teenagers didn't go to surgeons to look older, and all old people did was reminisce about their younger years. He liked that his soul was electric, lit by a fervor for life and charged by a lack of fear of death. The darkness surrounding what had happened in the hospital had dimmed that too. Joey wondered if he would ever be the same, if he wanted to be.

"Hey," Paige greeted as she opened the door and walked into Joey's room. "What are you doing?"

"Jerking off," Joey replied, unimpressed by his sister's intrusion. "You should've knocked."

"Wow, you're talented! I never knew people could masturbate with both of their hands behind their head. That's next level, Joey."

"Yeah, well, I've always been impressive."

Rolling her eyes, Paige sat on the end of his bed. "What's going on?"

"You're looking at it," he replied, displaying his hands in front of him to present the wonders of a room that had been raped of all electronics thanks to a Bridget on a mission.

There didn't seem to be much of a point to taking away Joey's television, PlayStation, and speaker system, but he knew it made his mother feel like she was doing something to punish his indiscretions. Realistically, all the boredom made him want to do was drugs. Perhaps that was why Bridget added the "You're never leaving the house" stipulation to the sentence. That one hurt more than expected. Typically, his mother would tell him he was on house arrest but let him out a day later, but after four days, Bridget wasn't budging.

Joey thought about sneaking out in an effort to assuage the claustrophobia he'd developed in captivity, but it wasn't worth it. Bridget had told him that his consequence for getting caught would be a month couch surfing in his Aunt Lauren's living room, and Joey didn't doubt her commitment to the threat.

Joey loved Lauren, but he didn't want to live among her four kids under six. Even the possibility of court-appointed rehab sounded like a better option.

"We got the official word this morning. Lilly's going to juvie for two months," Paige informed.

"She's lucky she's still seventeen."

"No doubt," Paige agreed. "One month later and she would've been super fucked."

"Well, lucky for her, Mattie went full bitch right from the jump,"

"Have you talked to her?"

"Nope. I'm sure I'll see her when I go back to work next week, but I'm not about to talk to the snitch."

"I don't blame you."

"I think Em's starting to."

Emily had spent the last handful of days trying get Joey to realize that Mattie had not purposely fucked Joey over, but it was no use. The fact that she'd run to the principal about someone selling was repulsive enough to Joey. There was no coming back from that. How could there be? It was everything they'd pushed back against for years. He didn't know what the crux of Mattie's issue with Lilly was, but it didn't matter. There was nothing she could say that would justify the actions she had taken. Emily disagreed—vocally. She'd been trying to push Joey into admitting that he would have done the same if someone he deemed an "enemy" was sitting in a spot that made it so easy to take a shot. He claimed that wasn't the case, but he was more confident in his words than he was in his heart.

When it came down to it, Joey knew Mattie's goal hadn't been to hurt him. He was a not-so-innocent bystander in a larger scheme that he didn't fully understand and wasn't sure he wanted to. It was petty as fuck, something he couldn't relate to in the least. He had never cared enough about anyone else's life to mess with it. The whole concept went against the live-and-let-live mantra he thought they all lived by. It was strange to see someone he thought he knew so differently, and it forced Joey to consider that he and his friends didn't understand each other the way he had thought they did. How could they? Mattie was making power plays that took Joey out by association, and Joey hid so much of himself from the people who were supposed to know him best. The secrets between them were mounting, and the space they caused was detrimental to the future of their friendships. In some ways, it seemed better to let the relationships go rather than acknowledge the insecurities and fears that drove the wedge.

Joey had never had a boyfriend, and he wasn't sure he wanted to if romantic relationships came with the same strain as other types. He hated drama that came from disappointing people he cared about and being disappointed by them in turn. He couldn't imagine how much more it would suck if he was actually in love with the person he was letting down.

"Emily doesn't think you should be pissed at Mattie?" Paige asked, crinkling her nose. "I don't understand that at all."

"I mean, she gets being pissed. She's mad too, but she thinks it was a misunderstanding."

Paige scoffed. "How could it be a misunderstanding? Even if she didn't intend for you to be collateral damage, she was good with messing with Lilly's life. That's, like, pathological."

"Pathological?" Joey smirked. "Is that what we're going with."

Shrugging, Paige gave Joey a grin. "I think so. It feels right. I like the way it rolls off the tongue."

"You do, huh?"

"Mm-hmm," she chuckled. "So what's going to happen with you?"

"You've asked me the same thing every morning, and I keep telling you I have no clue, Paigey."

"Like, are you supposed to go back to school on Monday?"

"We haven't heard anything yet, but I'm thinking that's a pretty obvious nope," Joey replied.

From what he understood through Bridget's conversations with administration, the school was deliberating next steps. Supposedly, the possibility of an arrest and various charges were still on the table. As much as Joey tried not to get worked up over potential outcomes, the idea of having to go to a juvenile detention center was formidable. He hated to be told what to do, and if he were incarcerated, he would be ordered around constantly, and there would be nothing he could do about it.

"Well, you had one good day back," Paige teased. "And that's really more than I expected."

"You're a savage," Joey laughed. "I thought I had at least three in me."

"Evidently, you were wrong."

"Dead wrong."

"The holidays are coming up," Paige noted.

"Yeah, so? What's your point?" Joey asked, narrowing his eyes at his sister. "I doubt they would hold off on locking me up because Thanksgiving is around the corner."

"That wasn't where I was going with this at all."

"Where were you going then?" he questioned, gnawing on his fingernails.

"You ruined it," she decided. "You got serious when I was about to make a joke and now I feel like an asshole going for it."

"It's literally never stopped you before," Joey reminded. "You love going for the guts."

Paige gave him a mischievous grin before standing and heading toward the door. "I guess we have that in common."

"You're really not gonna say what you were going to say?"

"I'm really not," she confirmed. "It had something to do with you getting coal in your stocking and it was super corny."

"That doesn't surprise me."

"And why's that?" Paige pressed, placing her hands on her hips. "I'm clever as fuck and you know it."

"Keep telling yourself that, P."

"I will," she assured.

"Good. And I'll keep telling you you aren't," Joey promised, laughing when Paige gave him the finger.

"Then you'll keep being wrong."

"Wrong?" Joey tsked. "I don't know anything about being wrong."

"Tell that to Principal Lloyd," Paige suggested as she exited the room.

Joey sighed and raked his hands through his hair. He didn't want to talk to Lloyd or anybody affiliated with the school district. If it were up to him, he would enroll in online school and be done with campus rules entirely. Maybe it was up to him, maybe he could finally be finished with waiting for decisions to be made about his life, maybe everything that happened was a force to push him in a different direction.

Settling into his pillow, he decided that the only decision he needed to make was the one that had him taking a morning nap. He had nothing better to do anyway.

## 25

Krista had insisted that Joey not be scheduled for at least a week after his incident. His boss promised that the decision wasn't intended to be a punishment but a responsible response to such a scary event. The time off was a blessing and curse. While shifts at the restaurant would give him something to do and help to lessen his boredom, he didn't have to see Mattie. He had been ignoring the onslaught of texts she sent and continued to ghost her until she gave up. Joey knew he was in for a marathon. His former friend wasn't one to readily admit defeat. It was a quality he used to admire in her, but the admiration had waned when Mattie debased herself to the level of teenage tattletale. The behavior was so unlike her, yet became less shocking when Joey recalled how much venom she had toward Lilly. He didn't understand it, but he couldn't pretend that he hadn't noticed it. Maybe if he had dug deeper, he could have gotten to the root of the issue. Unfortunately, he'd never cared enough to handle it, though he probably should have. Enduring the fallout hadn't piqued his interest either. He wasn't one to get involved in other people's bullshit, even if those people were his friends.

Interpersonal relationships were variable and treacherously

nuanced in ways Joey never felt fit to manage. It was easier to ignore the idiosyncrasies humans held than to learn them. He worried that his numbness was somehow detrimental to his life but figured the worry itself proved that he wasn't completely ignorant to what others were dealing with. It humanized him despite his concern that he lacked the typical emotions that other people dealt with.

Joey wondered if he'd been born tough or if he was made callous by the circumstances he'd had to cope with as a kid. He hated to blame his father for everything that went wrong in his life, but it seemed that his somewhat skewed perspective had burgeoned from a turbulent boyhood spent mostly sans dad.

"Are you going to give Mattie a chance to explain?" Emily asked as she lounged on Joey's bed.

Being on Bridget-mandated house arrest had turned Joey into the disgraced king of a crumbling kingdom. He accepted visitors in his stuffy room and entertained them in the least interesting ways. So much time spent locked away in his tower had caused his mind to wander to sexier activities he could participate in between the sheets. After months of deliberation, Joey finally made a profile on the hookup app he had been browsing. He knew lying about his age was questionable, but in the grand scheme of things, it wasn't his most egregious act. Joey wasn't sure, however, that the effort was worth it. The pickings were slim at best and he didn't want to be outed for fucking around with any of them. What happened in the dark always came to light, and he wasn't ready to show that side of him, especially when the risk didn't equal the reward. Still, the lack of options didn't stop Joey from serial swiping.

"That's not gonna happen," he replied, picking some lint off his sweatshirt to flick it at his friend. "So don't even ask me."

"Oh, I can't even ask you now?" Emily sighed, rolling her eyes. "Don't act like she did this to purposely hurt you when you know she didn't. She wouldn't. She had no idea it would affect you."

"If you're gonna keep playing lawyer, you can go," Joey said coolly.

He loved Emily, but he didn't covet anyone enough to put up with them telling him what to do. His distaste for authority spanned all forms, even when it was a friend thinking it was alright to bark bullshit in his ear. Joey barely listened to his mother, so he didn't know why anyone was delusional enough to think he would take direction from them. He wished he could live his whole life not being told what to do, be it by society, friends, or family. He wanted to be an autonomous entity who didn't answer to anyone, but he was pretty sure that the only way to be that person was to be alone. And he didn't think he wanted that either.

"Ugh," Emily groaned. "You're such a dick sometimes. This will tear us all apart, and you don't even care."

"I never said I didn't care," Joey stated. "I definitely care. I would rather it didn't happen at all, but it did, and now there's fallout. It is what it is."

"But it doesn't have to be the way it is," Emily whined. "C'mon. You know you're going to get over it eventually. Why don't you just speed up the process?"

"What difference does it make to you?"

Emily glared at Joey like he had ten heads. "All the difference in the world. Now, I have to split my time between the two of you instead of just chilling as a group. I feel like a kid whose parents got divorced, and they're fighting for custody. I'm stuck in the middle and it fucking blows."

"First of all, stop being so goddamn dramatic. Second, you can spend all your time with her if you want to. Don't feel like you have to come over. Do whatever you want."

"That's not the point and you know it," Emily tsked. "You're twisting everything around and it's really exasperating."

"I'm literally not worked up at all. I'm sitting here, and you're getting heated," Joey noted.

"Because you're purposely avoiding the real issue and it's driving me crazy."

"What's the real issue that I'm avoiding?"

"That what happened isn't worth losing a longtime friend over," Emily reasoned. "Seriously, you probably would've gotten kicked out of school anyway in a few days. It's how you function or don't function—whichever."

Unable to stop himself, Joey laughed at the statement.

"See," Emily grinned. "You know I'm right. And are you really going to pretend that you care that much about Pacific High or school in general? It's preposterous to even act like you do at this point."

"Spell preposterous," Joey ordered, smirking at his flustered friend.

"Honestly, you're so fucking annoying."

"Yet here you sit, begging to spend more time with me. You must like me enough."

"Or hate myself enough," she retorted with a wink, "either way. So …"

"So …?" Joey repeated, looking at his friend quizzically. She couldn't have been taking the conversation where he thought she might be taking it. Emily was smarter than that.

"Should we call Mattie and tell her to come over so you guys can squash this?" she asked, placing her hands together in prayer position.

"Absolutely fucking not."

Emily stared at him with eyes as big as saucers. "You're kidding, right?"

"Do I look like I'm kidding?" Joey questioned, ensuring the expression on his face reflected the fact that he was not.

"Not at all."

"Good, that's because I'm not."

"You're so stubborn," Emily chided, burying her face in her hands.

"And you're still so dramatic. You have to let it go. You're setting yourself up for disappointment."

"Why should today be different from any other day?" she said. "How are you going to handle work? You're going to be forced to see her. Are you going to ignore her?"

Shrugging, Joey reached for the bag of sour straws sitting on his bedside table. He offered the gummies to Emily before placing two between his lips. "What am I?" he asked, swinging them back and forth with a roll of his neck.

"An idiot."

"Ha, ha," he guffawed sarcastically. "You're the idiot. I am ... clearly a walrus."

"Yeah, no shit. Answer my question," Emily demanded.

"What was the question?"

"Are you going to ignore Mattie?"

"I'm ignoring you," Joey replied matter-of-factly. "That's my plan. You're relentless, so I'm gonna ignore you."

Yawning, Joey tucked the comforter around his neck and closed his eyes, a not-so-subtle indication that he was over the conversation. Emily's defense of Mattie's decisions was aggravating. The more she talked, the more frustrated Joey became. For the sake of their friendship, he had to tune her out.

"I'll drop it for a while, but I'm not going to give up. One day you guys will get back together," Emily stated, reaching under the blanket to tickle the bottoms of Joey's feet.

He laughed and kicked her playfully, trying to knock her off of the bed. "Get outta here!"

"Aw, the ticklish baby," Emily crooned, continuing her assault on his appendages. "You're not so tough now, are you?

They fell to the floor with a thud, giggling as they attempted to triumph in the tickle fight. Breathless and tired, they rolled away from one another, remaining on high alert.

"Truce, truce," Emily offered, holding her hand out for a shake.

Skeptically, Joey searched his friend's eyes to assess her seriousness. After determining that she was being genuine, he shook on it.

"See how easy it is to make amends," she wondered. "And it feels good, hm?"

Joey rolled his eyes as Emily squeezed his hand.

"Think about it, okay?" she pleaded. "I'm not asking you to make a decision right now. I'm just asking you to consider it."

He nodded as a means to shut her up. If she kept pushing, he would feel compelled to hold his ground. He'd never bent to the wind before and he wasn't going to start. Emily might have believed she could be a storm, carrying change with her, but Joey was solid as a boulder when it came to his decisions. He wasn't going to budge.

## 26

Joey had expected an arrest or expulsion for his foray into K2, both of which would have been less complicated than the outcome he received. While an expulsion remained on the table—and was highly likely—the arrest was staved off by the requirement that he check into a rehabilitation facility. Despite Joey's opinion that serving time in a juvenile detention center would be easier than doing a stint in rehab, Bridget wasn't having any of it. Though his mother would never admit it, Joey knew Bridget was thrilled with the promise of mandatory rehab. He'd even heard her and Steve whispering about what a blessing it was and how great it would be for him.

He couldn't think of anything he wanted to do less. The idea of being sober and forced into therapy several times a day was a fate worse than death. He would have much rather rotted in juvie with a bunch of other fuckups. At least he would have had like-minded people to chill with. He didn't want to do some Kumbaya, twelve-step bullshit. Rehab didn't work. It hadn't helped his father and it wasn't going to help him. He'd never be a person who could give himself to the process and expect results. It was bizarre that Bridget believed it could help him. She'd seen firsthand how useless it was, yet she held out hope that it would work for Joey. Realistically, Joey was aware that it was the delusions of a desperate mother. He hated that that was what he'd made Bridget into, but he couldn't stop living the life she'd given him just to please her. It was her fault anyway. She'd raised him to be strong and independent. The qualities didn't generalize based on who wanted him to have them. He was who he was, and he was confident that that was the only person he could be.

The only bright spot to rehab was that there wouldn't be a bed available for him. The holidays were quickly approaching and there was no way they were going toss a kid into a facility right before the most quintessential family time of the year.

"They have a bed for you," Bridget announced the day before Thanksgiving. "We're taking you up to Jennings on Friday."

"It's Black Friday," Joey cried. "We need to go to the mall. You have to tell them that we can't make it."

"I can't tell them that you can't make it," Bridget replied, scraping the remnants of a fried egg off the pan she was washing. "This isn't, like, a dinner date or something, Joey. This is mandatory."

"Wait," Paige began, her mouth full of breakfast. "If it's thirty days and he's going in on November 29th ... he's going to be in there for Christmas."

"I don't know how that's going to go," Bridget admitted.

"You don't know how that's going to go?" Joey questioned. "You're gonna let them take me over Christmas?"

"Mandatory," Bridget repeated. "That means no matter how much you want to, you don't make the rules. Mandatory is a good word for you to learn. No matter how much you want to be in charge of every aspect of your life, you're not going to be. That's not the way things work."

"I'm sure they give you some sort of leave," Steve added. "They're not going to keep kids away from their homes on Christmas."

"But it's okay to keep kids away from their home for the rest of the year?" Joey questioned.

"It's inhumane."

"It's a necessity," Steve corrected. "Nobody sends their kids there because they want to."

"You want me there," Joey challenged. "I heard you and Mom talking about it. You think it will be good for me."

"Oh, I'm not going to deny that," his stepfather confirmed. "You need it."

"*Need* it?" Joey scoffed. "I don't *need* rehab. It's a punishment, not a necessity. I'm not an addict." Though neither of them said a word, the look that Bridget and Steve shared spoke volumes about their disagreement. "You think I am?"

"I think you would benefit from the intervention," Bridget said slowly as if she had chosen her words carefully. "And the therapy."

"It would only do you good," Steve added. "There's nothing wrong with getting some help to deal with some of the hard stuff you've been through. Right now, it seems like you're leaning on drugs to cope with it all."

"Why would I need to go to therapy when I have a shrink sitting with me in the kitchen?" Joey snarked. "If you're so tapped in on the hard stuff I'm dealing with, tell me what it is."

Joey knew Steve was referencing his father—their complicated relationship and Jack's death—but Joey wasn't haunted by the past as much as he was uncertain of the present. Steve didn't know shit, nobody did. Maybe that was the biggest problem. Maybe everyone needed to find out that he was gay.

Maybe it would explain some of his decisions or, at the very least, shift the focus from the myriad of fucked up things he did enough for people to draw their own conclusions. He needed to change the narrative, show some vulnerability, and most of all, garner a little bit of sympathy. He'd never thought he would come out in an attempt to avoid rehab, but if it could save his ass, he wasn't opposed to taking the risk.

"I'm guessing there are a lot of things. I don't know specifically what they are, but you're a fifteen-year-old kid who lost your dad. That's not easy," Steve stated.

As annoyed as Joey should have been by Steve speaking like he knew what was going on, he couldn't be too peeved. Steve was caring, patient, and consistent. Joey couldn't imagine what his mother's life would be like if Steve weren't in it. Not only did his stepfather endure Bridget's idiosyncrasies, he put up with Paige and Joey's wild ways. Though Joey wasn't privy to many details about Steve's adolescence, he surmised that the older man had a bit of a debauched past. As far as Joey was concerned, the way that Steve remained mostly unfazed by Joey's antics supported the assumption.

"The bottom line is we want the best for you, and if rehab is part of the process, then it's a part of the process," Bridget explained, taking a seat beside Joey. "I can see you're struggling and I want to know why. Like, if we understand more, I can better support you. Supposedly, there's a family component to your therapy. We're expected to attend two sessions during your stay. Maybe it will be good for all of us."

Licking his lips in preparation to speak, Joey identified that Bridget had given him the perfect opening to tell her about his very specific struggle. All he needed to do was tell her that he was gay and the admission would possibly explain some of his behavior away. If Bridget and Steve believed Joey was tormented by his sexuality, they would have a greater understanding of the struggles they were so keen to reference. While he wasn't entirely sure that any of his behavior was caused by his closeted status, he knew it would be a piece of the puzzle his parents were looking to place.

Opening and closing his mouth like a fish combing water for food flakes, Joey attempted to find the words he wanted to say. He figured it could be as simple as "I'm gay," but regardless of how much he wanted to make the admission, the phrase stayed stuck on the tip of his tongue.

"What's up?" Bridget questioned skeptically. "You look like you have something to add."

"I do," Joey confirmed, clearing his throat and adjusting his posture. "I want to tell you something."

"Tell us," Bridget prompted, placing her hand on his knee supportively. "Whatever you have to say, just say it."

Joey narrowed his eyes, wondering what Bridget was angling at. "What do you think I'm going to say?"

She shrugged. "I don't know, but whatever it is, I want you to know I'm supportive."

"What if I'm about to tell you that I'm a serial killer and the bodies of six nuns are stacked in the basement," Joey wondered, raising an eyebrow. "What would you say about that?"

"What do you have against nuns?" Steve inquired, taking a bite of his toast. "That's an oddly specific statement. I feel like I need to go down to the basement and check."

"Maybe it's true," Joey smirked. "What would you say?"

"I would say we need to find a better place for the bodies," Bridget laughed.

"You would call the police," Steve disagreed. "We both would because we'd probably be next."

"I'm far from a nun," Bridget retorted. "And so are you. Seriously, baby, what's up?"

Joey hated himself for being so hesitant. There was no reason to be so scared, yet he was, and it enraged him. It wasn't that he was ashamed of his sexuality. It was more that he had held it so close to his chest, protected it for so long that it felt too strange to expose it. In not acknowledging it or speaking about it for years, Joey's sexuality had become bigger than he could handle.

"I want to go to a convent instead of rehab. I'm going to become a nun," he said, drawing rolled eyes from his parents.

"I guess your killer instincts would be well-served there," Steve reasoned.

Bridget sighed and moved her soothing hands off him. "Here I thought you were going to say something of substance. Really Joey, you should consider taking things seriously sometimes. It would serve all of us well."

"I'll pray on it," Joey joked as he rose from the table.

Divine intervention was the only type he needed. It would have been great if the universe gave him the strength not to be so chickenshit.

## 27

Constantly resting was surprisingly exhausting. The more time Joey spent lounging in bed, the more difficult it was to get out of his room. Even making his way outside to lay on the deck took a great deal of effort. Late November in Missouri wasn't exactly sunbathing weather, but the rays felt good on Joey's face. He wondered what it would be like to live in a place where it was warm all the time, where he didn't have to bundle in layers to be moderately comfortable. Though he wasn't crazy about the temperature, he had to admit the air was fresh in Pacific.

Rolling over on the bench, he repositioned himself onto his stomach so he could admire the beauty of the snow-covered yard. As much as he dreamed of living in California—or close to a beach—Joey knew he would miss the seasons. There was something magical about the way ice glistened on bare tree branches, catching the light and projecting prisms on the blanket of white below. If his fingers weren't frozen, he would have gotten his sketch pad out and started to draw. Though nature wasn't typically what inspired him to create, he loved the look of the land before him, how quiet and serene it was in comparison to his complicated life.

His hiatus from work, weed, and school— along with the

grounding of a lifetime from Bridget—had compelled Joey to find different ways to pass the time. It was instinctive that he went toward art. The release he achieved when he was dragging paint across paper or shading with a pencil was similar to what he experienced while he was high. It was freeing to be somewhere else for a while, to lose himself in geometric shapes or bold colors. Maybe he would have cared more about school if school cared more about the arts. It wasn't worth perseverating on what could have been. Systematic change without the promise of a monetary benefit for the system was a pipe dream—so Joey would hit the pipe rather than the books, living the dream. Or nightmare.

"It's freezing out here," Paige stated, drawing Joey's attention. He glanced over his shoulder to see his sister hugging her slim body. Though she was wearing an oversized sweater that could have housed a small family under its cover, her teeth were still chattering. "Come inside."

"I'm good," he replied, resting his forehead on the wood slats of the bench.

"Sure, people who are good always lay facedown on benches in frigid weather. You know who does that? People who don't have homes. You have one. Get inside it."

"I don't have one," Joey disagreed. "If I did, I wouldn't be forced out of it."

"For a month," Paige said. "It's a month, and you know damn well that all this shit is on you."

Joey sat up to face his sister. "It's kinda on Lilly too. She sold some wicked shit."

"Oh please," she huffed. "You're the dumbass who decided to smoke it before school. And who knew you'd have such a weird reaction?"

"I'm kidding, I don't blame her. I blame Mattie."

"I mean ..." Paige cringed. "As much as I want to, it's still on you."

"Yeah, I was half kidding about that too," Joey relented. He sighed and grudgingly rose to his feet when Paige gestured at the door.

Following his sister up to her bedroom, Joey silenced his phone.

The notifications he'd been receiving on the hookup app were out of control. He didn't need Paige to get curious about the constant buzzing.

Joey tossed himself onto Paige's bed. He had become so bored that any change of venue was moderately exciting.

"I'm upset about the whole rehab thing," Paige admitted, lying next to him. "It feels too familiar, you know?"

He nodded, too hesitant to find words for his thoughts.

"It never worked for Dad," she sighed. "Is there even a chance that it will for you? It's not that I don't have faith in you. I guess I don't trust the process."

"I don't need it like he did," Joey uttered. "He was reluctant, and he needed it. It's not like that for me."

"Says who?" Paige questioned. "From where I'm sitting, it's pretty obvious that you need the help."

"Maybe you need to find a different seat."

Rolling her eyes, Paige stated, "I'm serious."

"I'm not Dad. I'm so far from being like him ..." Joey paused, biting his tongue before continuing his thought. "In, like, a million different ways."

"I think you're wrong. The familiarities are super apparent, even if you don't want to acknowledge them."

"Whatever," Joey grumbled. He considered leaving Paige's room to lounge somewhere else, but it wasn't worth the bother.

"I'd love to know a few ways you think you're different from him," she prodded. "You said 'a million different ways' and I can't think of three."

"Really, Paige?" he tsked, hoping the daggers he shot from his eyes landed solely in her sense of reason.

Paige frowned as tears pooled on her waterlines. "I just want you to be okay. You're my little brother. I don't want to lose you."

Joey clicked his tongue. He hated emotionally charged conversations. They made everything overwhelming, no matter the topic. The weight of the discussion would have driven Joey to change the course of the discussion, but the care and concern rife on his sister's face prompted him to take it in a different direction.

Though he had intended to come out to Bridget several times during the prior weeks, Joey couldn't bring himself to do it. Every time he began to broach the subject, he aborted the mission before he could confess. The longer it took to make the admission, the more he doubted he would ever be able to. Maybe he would just start dating guys and never speak on it aside from introducing them to his family. He wasn't sure why he was such a wimp, but he had to get it together. He was running out of time for an explanation that might keep him out of rehab. Perhaps it would be easier to tell Paige and let her spread the word regarding his sexuality. It seemed easy enough—after all, his sister had a big mouth when she wasn't sworn to secrecy.

"You're not gonna lose me," Joey replied, tapping into the tenderness he naturally held toward Paige. "Honestly, there's just been a lot on my mind."

"There's been a lot going on," Paige reasoned. "It makes sense that you would be stressed. I know you like to believe that you don't let things get to you, but you are human. It would be weird if the stuff you've been through didn't impact you."

"It's not that," Joey began. "I mean, it is, but it's not. It's just …" He paused, silently admonishing himself for being such a bitch about a few words he'd been anxious about saying for so long. They were only words. He'd never been nervous to speak before, that was proven by years of report cards that indicated he was quite loquacious. Words, that was all they were, words he could say and move past, words he wouldn't let get the best of him. "I'm gay."

"Because you're nervous?" she asked, confused. "I just told you that it's totally normal to be nervous in these circumstances."

"Paige," he said slowly, in disbelief that he'd actually said the phrase and annoyed he had to say it again, "I'm literally gay."

The subsequent look on Paige's face revealed her realization of what Joey had said. "I never thought you would tell me that."

"Because you thought I wasn't or …"

"No, I mean, I knew you were, but I never thought you'd say it just like that. You've always been really secretive about who you have crushes on and stuff."

"Wait," Joey insisted, putting his hand up for emphasis. He couldn't believe what Paige had said. She'd *known* he was gay. He'd put forth a good amount of effort to make sure people didn't, and she just *knew*. "You knew I was? How?"

"I don't know. I just did."

"Wow."

"Are you upset about it?" Paige asked, reaching over to rub his upper arm.

"About what? Being gay or you knowing I was and never saying anything about it?"

She shrugged. "I don't know—either?"

"Kinda," he admitted, not positive which option he was referring to.

"What was I supposed to say? I didn't want to insult you."

"You think it's an insult?" Joey knew what Paige meant, but his frazzled nerves had him on the defensive. Bringing his index finger to his teeth, he worked on his nail bed.

"Don't even go there," she chided. "You know what I meant."

"Yeah," Joey sighed, wondering if his mother had the same insight Paige did. "Hmm, that was easier than I expected."

"Oh," Paige said thoughtfully. "Good. I'm glad."

"Do you think Mom and Steve would believe that my inner confusion made me do the stuff I did and now that I came to terms with it, I don't need rehab?"

"Do you really think that's why you acted the way you did?" she asked carefully. "Because you've been lashing out or something?"

"Who knows! I'm not a therapist," Joey cried, taking a break from his nail-gnawing to crinkle his nose skeptically. "I'm just asking if you think they'll buy it."

"Are you seriously leveraging your coming out as a way to get out of rehab?"

"Um, yeah," Joey replied matter-of-factly.

Paige scoffed. "I thought you were really nervous about this."

"I am, but I'm not gonna do it for nothing. If I didn't think there could be a benefit from admitting it, I wouldn't have."

"Maybe the benefit would be that you're accepting yourself for who you are and decreasing the amount of stress you hold inside."

"Okay, yeah, that too," he said, waving off her psychobabble. "You should tell Mom, make it seem like I'm too scared to tell her."

"Are you?"

"I was," Joey answered. Paige's easy acceptance had assuaged his anxiety immensely.

"But now you're not?"

"I don't know. It doesn't matter," he answered impatiently. All the avoidance he'd done regarding the admission made him impatient for it to get done while he had the nerve—and a reason. "Are you going to help me out or not?"

Paige nodded and gave Joey a fake grin. "I guess I am."

"Go team," Joey said, smiling back at her.

The best-case scenario was that Bridget and Steve would do what they could to help him avoid rehab. He didn't need it anyway.

## 28

Joey insisted that Paige give him a verbatim re-enactment of Bridget's reaction to the news and after his sister complied, he made her do it again.

"And then what did she say?" Joey questioned, sitting on the edge of his bed and bouncing his knee nervously as he awaited the response he already knew.

"She asked why it was coming from me and not from you."

"And you said ..." he prodded.

"Fuck, you're annoying," Paige groaned, rubbing her forehead.

"You didn't say that to Mom."

His sister let out an exasperated sigh and glared at Joey, unimpressed. "I said that to you."

"You're not supposed to be talking to me, you're supposed to be going through your conversation with Mom again. Every single word, like I told you before," Joey demanded, glancing at the packed suitcase leaning against the threshold of his open bedroom door.

He was scheduled to leave for the rehabilitation center in less than an hour, and though his plan was in motion, there didn't seem to be any stalling. It had been twenty minutes since Paige had told Bridget that Joey was gay and his mother had yet to come to his room.

He wondered what she was doing. Maybe she was more upset than he had expected her to be, more disappointed. As tentative as he'd been to come out to his mother, he had never thought the admission would make her think of him differently or love him less. It was strange to even consider that a dip in her affection could actually happen.

"I said that you were worried," Paige answered. "That you were scared of how she'd react."

"That must have annoyed her," Joey noted. If there was one thing Bridget was, it was open-minded, even alluding to her having an issue with his sexuality had to have pissed her off.

"Like I told you before, it did."

"Then why hasn't she come in here."

"Why haven't you gone in there?" Paige retorted. "It should've come from you to begin with.

This whole harebrained plan is stupid."

"It's easy to say it's stupid when it's not working," Joey stated.

"I told you it was dumb before," she reminded, tucking her hands into the pocket of her hoodie, "and as usual, you didn't listen."

"Whatever," he grumbled, scrolling through the social media apps on his phone. It was daunting to think that he would lose custody of his device when he walked through the doors of the rehabilitation center. Of all the horrible things he would have to endure there, Joey was sure that was the worst. Being cut off from the world wouldn't help him in the least. It was calming to him to have access to funny videos or viral memes. It was a way to stay plugged in while tuning out and an escape that he turned to more than weed or any other drug.

"Are you packed and ready to go?" Bridget asked as she sidestepped the luggage partially blocking her way.

Joey froze in place, eyes locked on his mother's, heart beating fast. "Huh?"

Bridget's hair was wrapped in a towel and she was wearing her pink terry bathrobe. "I see your suitcase is done, but do you have all of your toiletries?" she continued. "Why are you looking at me like that?"

"Like what?" Joey asked, taken aback by his mother's nonchalance.

"Like you're confused," she answered.

"Because I am," he confessed.

"If it's about what your sister told me, I wish you had been the one to come to me," she began, moving closer to him. "And you should already know that I love and accept you regardless of who you're interested in."

Joey didn't expect anything different, but he was hoping for some long heart-to-heart talk that made heading to the facility that afternoon an impossibility. "That's it?"

"Not at all," Bridget answered, leaning down to give Joey a hug as he sat motionless. "I figured we'd have lots of time to talk on the way to Jefferson City."

"Shouldn't we talk here instead of in the car?" Joey asked, his voice getting higher as panic rose in his throat. It didn't work. His mother still planned on taking him to rehab. He thought they would sit on the couch eating some fucking Chinese food and talking about boys. He thought Bridget would pet his head while he lay on her lap. She would tell him how brave he was and try to understand the struggles everyone assumed he coped with. Though Joey knew he struggled, it was hard to pinpoint how. He didn't think his whole messy life was a reaction to his sexuality and the secret he had made it, even if that was what he wanted his mother to believe—at least in the short-term.

"We have to get you to Jefferson City by four for check-in," Bridget replied. "They're not going to be impressed if you're late, and there's a lot riding on your participation in the program."

"Like what? What's riding on this?" Joey cried. The admission of his sexuality being trumped by a random stint in rehab was baffling.

"Your sobriety," Paige offered, yelping when Joey chucked a pillow at her. "What? It's a fair statement."

"I meant something that matters," Joey amended.

"Well, sobriety definitely matters," Bridget interjected, "in general and specifically in regard to your freedom and future at PHS."

"I wouldn't say I'm *free* when I'm locked in rehab."

"It's better than having a record and doing time in juvie," his mother reminded, "because that's the other option."

"You have to get over the idea that he's going to get back into school, Mom," Paige tsked.

"There's no way that's going to happen."

"Well, Principal Lloyd gave me some hope," Bridget replied, "and I'm intent on keeping any shred of it I can get my hands on."

"He said it would look good to the board that I was getting help. That's hardly a ringing endorsement. They're going to expel me. It's a given."

"Shush," Bridget hushed, placing her finger on Joey's lips. "It's hard enough that I have to take you there today. Don't make it worse."

"It doesn't seem like it's that hard," Joey pouted. "You said it yourself that we have a lot to talk about, and you're rushing me out of the house."

"As happy as I am that you're living your genuine life and being open, it isn't lost on me that you decided to bring it up the day I have to take you to Horizons," she noted, smirking at him. "I think you thought that I'd hold off on checking you in."

"It seemed like a safe assumption," he said, garnering a laugh from his mother and sister.

"I told you it wouldn't happen. It wasn't exactly a subtle approach, so I guess it was pretty much on par with everything else you do," Paige teased.

"My baby's as subtle as a sledgehammer," Bridget chuckled, kissing Joey's cheek. "Make sure you have everything and meet me downstairs in fifteen. We can stop for hot chocolate before we hit the highway and have a talk."

"I'm not talking about it in public," Joey stated, crossing his arms over his chest.

"You've never been embarrassed by anything in your life," Bridget said, tussling Joey's hair much to his chagrin. "You're not going to start now. I'm not saying you should tell everybody before you're ready; I'm just saying you don't have anything to be ashamed of. I hope you know that."

"I'm not ashamed," Joey bristled. At least, he didn't think he was. "I'm just confused."

"About your sexuality?" Paige questioned.

"No, I'm gay as fuck," he answered. "I'm confused about why you're taking me to rehab even after I had this major breakthrough."

"Because you'll have even more breakthroughs there," Bridget replied. "You'll go for a month and come back a new kid."

"And that's what you want, huh? For me to be a new kid."

Bridget shook her head. "That's not the case and you know it. I want you to be the you that you are when you're not high. The Joey who makes good decisions."

"That Joey has never existed," Paige snarked. "Like, I'm all for this sparkles and rainbow shit, but let's be a little bit realistic."

"And you're a pillar of good decision-making?" Bridget challenged.

Joey laughed, giving his mother a nod of approval. "Savage, Mom."

"Savage and untrue," Paige fumed, rolling her lips in tight as she gave her mother a dirty look.

"Ugh, now I pissed her off," Bridget sighed, walking out of the room. "Fifteen minutes," she called from halfway down the hallway.

"Bitch," Paige grumbled.

"Yeah, you are," Joey stated, garnering a middle finger from his sister. "You have nothing to complain about. You're not getting shipped off to rehab."

Paige softened, resting her hand on Joey's, "You're going to be, like, an hour away and it's only thirty days. You'll be fine."

"I know I'll be fine," he grunted, staring at his suitcase. It was unbelievable that he was going. He already couldn't wait to be home. "I'm always fine."

"Is that so?" she asked. Her intonation made the question less abrasive than it could have sounded.

"It's so," he promised.

"I'll miss you," Paige crooned, giving Joey a tight hug. "Shit will be boring around here without you."

"There's no doubt about that," Joey said, hugging her back. She smelled like orange blossoms and vanilla. He'd miss the scent of her shampoo in the bathroom and her crazy-ass antics—even when they had him naked, picking up toilet paper rolls in the kitchen.

How would he survive a month without his family? It was awful to even consider not being with them for Christmas. People insisted that rehab wasn't a punishment, but it felt like one to Joey. And for the first time in a long time, he was given a punishment that actually hurt.

## 29

The ride to rehab was sweet and that made the arrival that much more bitter. It was a relief for Joey to talk to Bridget about the him he shared with so few people. He was happy to let his mother in fully, but it felt like too little too late. As soon as he was *out*, he was in the rehabilitation facility, locked behind its brick walls for weeks, learning things about himself he would never divulge to anyone.

The work was hard, and it never stopped feeling like a punishment. Joey spent the majority of his days wishing he were anywhere else, dreaming of the alternate consequence of juvenile detention, pining for home. Though he had been wrong about many things, Joey was right about the fact that the rehab's administration wasn't callous enough to keep kids from being with their families on Christmas. He was granted a twenty-four-hour leave to celebrate the holiday, an allowance that felt like a blessing and a curse. Joey knew the short period of time at home would make him miss it even more immensely than he already did. While it wasn't a case of out of sight, out of mind, Joey found it easier to attempt to forget what he was missing rather than get lost in it—even when his brain was intent on doing the latter. New memories would only make the task of disregarding his homesickness more difficult. Still, there was no way he was going to give up the chance to see his family. The once-weekly visits with Bridget, Steve, and Paige weren't enough. As much as he tried to do his own thing and considered himself to be independent, he was only empowered because he had them behind him.

Group therapy reminded Joey of what an anomaly he was. Most of the teens in treatment lacked familial support or family in general. Some of them had pushed their parents to their limits, and others had parents who were too far gone themselves to recognize how their children were struggling. It made Joey wonder what his life would have been like if his father hadn't died, a train of thought that was probably supposed to lead to a series of epiphanies but caused an ache in his stomach instead. Though he would never admit it to Paige, Christmas was a difficult time for him just as it was for her. He didn't think fondly of his father the same way his sister did, but that didn't mean he was numb to nostalgia. He was guilty of imagining how things could have been if everything had been different. Pondering the past didn't do much but make him wary of the future, worried about what his path would eventually become if it were paved in mistakes similar to those his father had made.

"We're so excited to have you home," Bridget said for what Joey estimated to be the twentieth time since he'd gotten into the car for his day away from the facility.

"So you've said," Joey replied, gazing out the window at the miles of white beyond it.

Large flakes fell heavy from the snow-bloated clouds and accumulated on the windshield as the wipers worked to brush it off. The rhythmic squeak lulled him to sleep and Joey woke up confused when the car parked in the driveway.

Bridget grinned as he looked at her through sleepy eyes. "I'm glad you got a nice nap. We have a lot to do."

The statement irritated him initially, but Joey was happy when he realized that the work entailed helping to trim the Christmas tree, an activity his family had held off on doing until he got home. In prior years, Joey hadn't been into decorating, but it held more weight after he'd been gone for so long. It was as if the holiday didn't truly start until he came home, like he was an integral part of the season if he was absent from a large share of the festivities.

Christmas at the Mills/Reegan house was always a big party with aunts, uncles, and cousins crowding the rooms. There was laughter and games, drinks and a ton of food. Traditionally, Joey was in charge of making the macaroni and cheese. He'd been recreating his great-grandmother Mills' recipe since his Aunt Hannah taught it to him when he was eleven. It was full of perfectly cooked noodles, provel cheese, and calories—everyone loved it.

"The mac and cheese man is back in action!" Joey's cousin Fallon crooned, giving him a hug from behind as he stirred the pasta.

"Hey Fal," he greeted, pinching cayenne pepper between his fingers and sprinkling it onto the food. "How's it going?"

"Better now," she smirked, plucking a noddle from the pot. "I'm starving, and you're cooking. I can't think of a better combination."

"Well, I'm home and you're here. That's a pretty good one too," Joey replied, smiling at her.

"You look cute," he noted, "I like the fur."

"It's faux," Fallon said, hitting her best Vogue poses in the bright pink coat she was wearing.

"Really? I couldn't tell from the color," Joey teased, laughing as Fallon tickled his side.

He loved Fallon's wild style, both in fashion and in life. She was a freshman at St. Louis University who always did well in school while continuing to be fun as hell.

"Touché," she giggled, going for another bite of macaroni. "So, how's rehab?"

"It fucking sucks."

She cringed. "That bad?"

"I doubt anyone's ever answered that question in a positive way," Joey reasoned. "I can't wait to get out of there for good."

"How much longer do you have to stay?" Fallon inquired, giving up on making the mac and cheese a finger food and going for a spoon.

Joey laughed as his cousin ate straight from the pot.

"It's so good," she garbled, her mouth full of macaroni.

"Thanks."

"How long do you have to stay there?" Fallon repeated.

"Another ten days. I'll get home a little after New Year's."

"What a way to ring it in, huh?" Fallon tsked. "Do yourself a favor and stay out of there in the future."

Joey nodded. "Oh I'm planning on it. There's no way I'll ever go back."

"You're going back," Bridget interjected, accepting the bite Fallon held out for her. "Mmm, it's yummy, Joey."

"I was talking about after this time," Joey corrected, "and good. I'm glad I've still got it."

"You definitely do," his mother confirmed, tugging him down so she could plant a kiss on his forehead. "You have to stop growing."

"He has like five inches on you already," Fallon chuckled. "You're in trouble, Aunt Bridge.

This cutie's going to break a lot of girls' hearts."

Bridget glanced at Joey who looked back at her and then regarded his cousin. "Boy's hearts," he stated.

"Boys ..." Fallon began, confused. It took a moment before Joey saw the light turn on in her head. "Boys!" she exclaimed. "Boys! Yay, you're gay!"

"Shh," Joey admonished, his eyes darting around the room to make sure nobody had heard. "It's not public yet."

"Why not?" she cried, pinching Joey's cheeks so she could look him directly in the face.

"This is amazing. I thought you were cool before, but this is next level."

"Because I'm into guys?" Joey asked, perplexed by Fallon's excitement.

"I mean, kind of I guess. It's more that you're young, strong, progressive, and gorgeous. You're everything everyone in our generation wants to be. You have it all."

Bridget's eyes were wide as she nodded along with what Fallon was saying, and when Joey peeked at his mother, they both began to laugh.

"You have nothing to be ashamed of," Fallon insisted.

"I'm not ashamed of who I am," Joey promised. "Not at all."

"Then tell the world," she urged. "Live your truth, and show everyone what a fucking force you are."

"And here I thought you were just fired up about the macaroni and cheese," Joey uttered as his cousin dropped her hands from his face and went back to scarfing the side dish.

"Oh hell no, not after you come forward with that kind of information."

While Joey never expected Fallon to have a problem with his sexuality, he didn't think she would be so goddamn elated. It was odd and endearing in the same way his cousin was. Without the ability to control his thoughts, Joey's mind wandered to what Emily and Mattie would think of his news. Would they be as over the moon as Fallon was? Would they be completely unsurprised like Paige? Would they be unconditionally supportive like Bridget? Thinking about Mattie instantly put him in a bad mood. He chided himself for consistently lumping her into his considerations. He only had one night at home. He wasn't going to allow ruminations of an old friendship to tarnish the time. In the past, Emily and Mattie would have come over for dessert and played "money grab" with Joey's family. He was sure Emily would still come over and convinced that he would kick Mattie out if she showed up. His former friend had sent sporadic texts during his time in rehab, all of which he had seen when he got his phone back when Bridget checked him out for the holiday. Mattie continued to be incredibly apologetic and Joey continued to not care —even the isolation of rehab couldn't change that.

"This is the best Christmas ever," Fallon declared. "Don't you think so, Aunt Bridge?"

"I do," Bridget replied, smiling at Fallon and Joey.

Joey grinned back. He did too.

## 30

The evening only got better after dinner was served. The smell of fir and cinnamon mingled with the giggles that floated through the air, spreading the Christmas spirit to every corner of the house. With his belly and heart full, Joey cuddled next to Bridget on the couch to watch his family members attempt to get money out of tightly wrapped packages with oversized oven mitts on their hands. Joey's side hurt from the peals of laughter he succumbed to as a result of the spectacle.

"You look way more incapacitated than everyone else, Paige," Joey taunted, shaking his head at his sister's piss-poor performance. She could barely hold the box in her grip, let alone open it.

Paige held a mittened hand up and announced, "I'm giving you the finger. I know you can't see it, but it's there."

"I'll take your word for it," Joey smirked. He sighed when Paige continued her awful attempt. "Try something different. Throw an elbow into it or your teeth."

"I'm not tearing it apart with my teeth," Paige cried as if the advice was absurd. She paused and turned to Steve, who was observing the scene with amusement apparent on his face. "How much is in here?"

"I think it's a hundred and twenty," their stepfather stated. The news earned excited expressions from the entire extended family.

"You better believe I'm going to get my mouth all up in there when it's my turn," Fallon announced, chuckling when Paige brought the package up to her lips.

"How many times do you think Fal's said that same thing?" Joey joked, garnering a smack on the arm from his unimpressed mother. "What?"

"It's funny," Fallon grinned. "Especially since I'm so far from a mouth whore. I get lockjaw way too easily."

"I'm going to add that to the list of shit I never needed to hear about my daughter," Joey's Uncle Jim uttered as he stood and held up his empty glass. "Does anyone else need more eggnog?"

"I think it's about time to give up on the eggnog and move onto the harder stuff," Steve suggested, leading Jim into the kitchen.

"It's hard for parents to see their children as sexual beings," Fallon stated. "We spent a while talking about that in my sociology class this semester. It was actually really fascinating."

"Sounds like it," Paige mumbled as she tried to tear the tape with her teeth. From the way she was struggling, Joey could tell the mitts made it nearly impossible for her to hold the box up to her face. He studied her form in hopes that he'd have a chance to wage his own attack.

Keeping with his tradition of getting screwed in every game the family ever played, Joey had picked damn near the last number. The probability that someone else would get the money before he had the chance to compete was high.

"Twenty seconds left," Aunt Lauren warned. "And if you don't get it, your mama is about to show you how it's done."

"True that," Bridget agreed, smiling at her sister.

"Nobody says 'true that' anymore,'" Paige admonished.

"Keep wasting time talking shit," Bridget suggested. "You're just giving me a greater opportunity to get it done."

"Bridget's coming for everyone's necks tonight," Fallon declared, clapping her hands. "The Mills/Reegan branch on our family tree is officially the most iconic."

"Agreed," Joey confirmed.

"Time's up," Lauren announced. "Give it a go, Fal."

"Fuck," Paige grumbled, taking the mitts off to hand them to Fallon.

"Get it, cuz," Joey stated, barely glancing up from the phone that had demanded his attention.

It was strange to be tethered to his phone again. He knew time away from social media would feel like a vacation to some, but to him it was purgatory. Joey didn't particularly care what other people were up to, but he liked to be able to browse through their lives without being invested. It was escapism, and he liked the break.

*Emily (9:21pm): I have a cold.*

*Joey (9:21pm): Bitch, you're going to let some boogies get in the way of money grab? What's wrong with you?*

*Emily (9:22pm): The cold. It's brutal.*

*Joey (9:22pm): Whatever.*

*Emily (9:22pm): I miss you.*

*Joey (9:23pm): I miss you too. Come give me your cold. Maybe they won't send me back if I'm sick.*

*Emily (9:23pm): What are the chances that's gonna happen?*

*Joey (9:24pm): Doubtful at best. I'm fucked.*

*Emily (9:24pm): Is it awful?*

*Joey (9:25pm): It's not great.*

*Emily (9:25pm): But you'll be home for good soon. Only another week, right?*

*Joey (9:26pm) 10 days.*

*Emily (9:26pm): It will be over before you know it.*

*Joey (9:27pm): False.*

Joey was aware that Emily was doing her best to make him feel better, but he couldn't help but be annoyed by the positivity. Even though his friend couldn't possibly understand what he was going through, all he wanted her to do was acknowledge how much it sucked and not pretend it didn't.

*Emily (9:27pm): What time do you leave tomorrow?*
*Joey (9:27pm): 9am*
*Emily (9:27pm): If I feel better, I'll swing by to say hi.*
*Joey (9:28pm): Sounds good. Feel better.*
*Emily (9:28pm): Thanks. Love you! Merry Xmas.*
*Joey (9:29pm): Love you too.*

Uncle Jim patted Joey's shoulder as he walked behind the couch with his refilled drink. "Are you gonna be present or are we going to continue to compete with your phone?"

"I've only been on it for, like, five minutes," Joey defended. "I'm present."

"I'm just giving you shit," Jim said, grinning at Joey. "All the kids are obsessed with those things. It's generational at this point."

"And it's generational that old dudes feel compelled to comment on it," Fallon teased as she gnashed her teeth into the package. "This isn't gonna happen."

"You might actually get a crack at it, Joey," Bridget whispered, waggling her eyebrows as Joey smiled. "You'll be rich."

"Loaded," Joey joked. "It'll be great for the commissary. I could buy so many Gobstoppers; I'll be the most popular kid in rehab."

"I figured you already were," his mother said, pushing his hair off of his forehead. "Look at this face. I missed it." She planted a smooch on his cheek before standing up. "I'm getting more wine. Do you want another soda?"

"I'll take a beer," he replied easily, smirking at the expression on his mother's face.

She chuckled and shook her head. "You're a nervy little shit. Do you know that?"

"So I've been told," Joey answered, adding "often" when his mother continued to stare him down.

"Mm-hmm," she hummed, picking up her glass from the ground and crossing the room to retrieve Lauren's.

"Every year I think it will be *my* year and it never is," Fallon pouted, tossing herself onto the couch next to Joey. "I miraculously forget how difficult it is."

"Christmas is known for its miracles," Joey shrugged. "Yours is the joy of forgetting."

"That would be the best name for a song," Fallon's younger brother, Fisher, exclaimed from a few chairs away. "Is it cool if I use it?"

"Yeah, that's fine," Joey replied, urging his eyes not to roll out of their sockets.

Fisher shouldn't have bothered Joey as much as he did, but there was something about his wannabe-hipster cousin that got on Joey's last nerve. The sixteen-year-old consistently strove to be someone he wasn't, and though Joey knew he had a lot of bad qualities, he was glad to be authentic. Unlike Fisher, Joey never tried to be someone he wasn't. The good, the bad, the flaws; he was himself—in most ways.

Maybe Fallon secretly thought the same of Joey after finding out he was gay and reluctant to come out publicly. Maybe she found him to be inauthentic in the same way Joey thought Fisher was. Maybe everyone who knew the truth thought Joey was fake. It was crazy to consider that anyone would question his realness, but he couldn't fool himself into denying that perhaps he would have if he were on the outside looking in.

Gay kids stayed in the closet because they feared backlash from their families, friends, or church, none of which concerned Joey anymore. His family's acceptance made him less worried about anyone else's. There was no reason for him to purport to be someone he wasn't, and the added cushion of his pending expulsion made it easier for Joey to take the leap.

Toggling to Facebook, Joey perused handfuls of happy holiday pictures, liking and commenting on a few and moving quickly past the others. Everybody looked shinier and more content in front of a sparkling tree or wearing ugly Christmas sweaters. He smiled when Paige's picture appeared in his feed. The photograph was as dysfunctional as they were, with Bridget laughing into Steve's cheek while he stuck out his tongue at the camera. Paige was giving her cheesiest grin as Joey smirked at the lens and Nicole attempted to smize. The glimmer in their eyes reflected the excitement of the moment and comfort with the company. Taking a screencap, Joey cropped the image and saved it as his lock screen.

He hesitated before navigating back to the app, wondering if the support he felt at home was giving him a false sense of security. What was the worst thing that could happen?

With trembling fingers, he drafted the post, intent on making it as straightforward and concise as possible:

*Merry Xmas. I thought you should all know I'm gay.*

There. He stared at the screen for a moment, debating whether he should actually hit post or if he needed to elaborate in some way. He wasn't one for paragraphs, that was for sure, but he felt as though he should have said more.

Deleting the first draft, he tried again:

*I hope your holiday is merry and gay, like me.*

"What are you laughing at?" Paige asked, craning her neck to peek over his shoulder.

"I'm coming out on Facebook."

"You're doing what?" she gasped. "Really?"

Joey nodded. "What? Do you think I shouldn't?"

"No! I never said that. I'm surprised, but so, so, so proud of you," she said. "So proud. Let me see." Paige grabbed the phone out of Joey's hand and groaned at the post. "You can't do that. It's not even funny."

"It's funny," Joey disagreed. "I'm funny."

She shook her head and frantically began typing. When she handed the phone back to him, he assessed her work:

*I was worried about this moment, but I want to let you guys know that I'm gay. This shouldn't change anything.*

"That's fucking awful," he admonished, grimacing at his sister.

Sighing, he decided to give it one more try:

*I don't care what you say. I'm happy and I'm gay.*

He gestured to the screen and awaited Paige's reaction. Her teary-eyed nod confirmed that he had hit it on the head.

And when he finally hit post, he didn't regret it at all.

## 31

The influx of messages Joey received after his post had him wondering if he had reached some previously unattainable level of teenage popularity. The outpouring of support and excitement was as staggering as it was unexpected. People he hadn't heard from in years and those who he barely knew reached out to tell him what an inspiration he was, how proud they were. It would have been idyllic if it weren't for the flip side of the coin. For every ten cheerleaders, there was one asshole who felt it necessary to make threats or off-color jokes. Joey had expected those reactions to be the most prevalent and he was grateful that they weren't, but seeing the hatred and ignorance in real-time was daunting. The same guys who had congratulated him for evading expulsion were dragging him online. It was fucked up how fickle people could be but not surprising. There was something so fragile about a straight man's sexuality, something that drove them to put down men who didn't want women the way that they did. Though Joey was aware that there were guys who tolerated homosexuality, he didn't think many accepted it. Clearly, a faction of jerks at his former high school didn't. It could have been worse, and Joey knew that it wasn't worth perseverating over the few fuckers who were intent on making it that way.

Deciding he'd had enough of the positive and negative feedback, Joey turned his phone to silent. He was about to place it on his bedside table and close his eyes, when he saw yet another incoming call from Emily. He'd ignored the first dozen because he was busy with family and constant notifications, but he figured it was time to have a conversation that had been a long time coming.

"Helloooo," Joey sang into the phone, "shouldn't you be resting?"

"I should be, and I would have been if I hadn't just spent the last two hours trying to get ahold of you," Emily admonished.

"You sound like shit," Joey noted, cringing at how nasal her voice was.

"I told you I was sick," she reminded. "I wasn't exaggerating. Why are we even talking about this? Was your Facebook hacked or did I really not know this about my best friend?"

"Paige and my mom claimed they knew before I told them. You didn't have any idea?"

"That you were gay?" Emily questioned. "No, not at all. I just figured you weren't into any of the girls at school."

Joey laughed softly. "Well, that's true, but I'm not into any of the boys either."

"Really? Why not?"

"Are you?"

"Am I what?" Emily asked.

"Are you into any of the boys at our school?" he asked, pulling the comforter up around his neck.

"Not really."

"So ... same."

"But you *are* into guys," she clarified.

"One hundred percent," he confirmed.

"You've never been attracted to girls? Like, I've heard you make comments about girls before, was that for effect or something?"

"I mean, I can recognize when a girl's hot, but it doesn't mean I want to fuck one."

"Right, I can too," Emily uttered as if she was trying to work through her confusion. "Wait," she began, "Are you really a virgin or are you, like, fucking guys on the side and just not talking about it?"

Joey rolled his eyes and tilted his head back, urging himself to be patient. "I'm actually a virgin."

Emily's loud exhale made Joey chuckle despite himself. "Thank fuck. I thought I was the last one left."

"I'm pretty sure I'll be a virgin for life or at least for as long as I stay in Pacific. There are literally no hot guys around here," Joey stated. There had been countless times that he'd wanted to talk to his friends about mundane shit like how dry the well of prospective hookups ran in Pacific, but he had consistently stopped himself. What would have been considered a normal exchange between friends had always been off limits for him. As weird as it was to actually participate in the conversation, it was nice.

"None!" Emily agreed emphatically. "Except for you, of course."

"You don't have to gas me up when we're talking about guys," Joey promised. "Rag on dudes all you want. I'll agree. No caveats needed."

"This is a whole new day for our relationship," Emily laughed. "I can't believe I never even suspected. I probably should have suspected."

"It's probably better you didn't."

Joey didn't want to get into the danger of subscribing to stereotypes since he knew Emily wasn't one to compartmentalize people. The fact that she was surprised by his sexuality was slightly confusing to him after hearing his mother and sister undoubtedly confirm that they were aware before he so much as muttered the admission. Did they really know him that much better than his friends? Joey's mind began to drift to Mattie, curious if the text messages he had received from her a few hours before relayed her authentic shock or if she was playing up her surprise to draw a response from him. Regardless of the intention, Joey didn't reply.

"I wasn't trying to ..." Emily trailed off and then pivoted. "What did your mom say?"

"She's known since before I went to rehab."

"I'm trying not to be hurt by that," Emily admitted. "Why didn't you think you could tell me before now? You had to have known it wouldn't make me love you any less. Honestly, it probably makes me love you more."

"Oh yeah? Why's that?" he inquired, amused by the confession.

"Because you get me way better than I could've ever imagined you did before. When I bitch about guys, you don't take it personally, right? You agree with it."

"Usually," Joey confirmed. "Men are garbage."

"They are!" Emily cried. "You get it."

Giggling into his top sheet, Joey agreed, "I do. I could tell you some stories …"

"When?" Emily demanded. "I want those stories!"

"Maybe someday."

"Someday as in ten days?"

"Probably then," Joey confirmed. "Ugh, I can't believe I have to go back there. It's so fucking brutal."

"I can't wait until you're back for good. Not just for the boy talk, either. I miss you."

"I miss you too."

"Do you know who else misses you?" Emily began. Joey knew where she was going with the question; it was where she always ended up since his falling out with Mattie.

"Don't go there," Joey warned.

"She called me tonight after your post. She's dying to talk to you, Joey. She said she texted and as usual, you didn't reply."

"You would think she'd be used to it by now."

"Maybe you'll feel differently once you're out of rehab, when you can put this whole thing behind you once and for all," Emily said hopefully. "Then everything can go back to normal."

"Nothing will ever be normal again," he stated. "Things are different, and that's the way it is."

"Maybe you're the one who's different," Emily offered.

"Or maybe it's Mattie," Joey retorted.

"It could be both of you."

"Whatever," Joey grumbled, resting his eyes. "I'm going to sleep."

"Okay. I'm proud of you, Joey. It took a lot of courage to do what you did tonight," Emily complimented. "Hopefully I'll catch you before you leave tomorrow."

"Alright," he replied, hoping she didn't show up in the morning. The last thing he wanted to talk about before he headed back to Horizons was his defunct friendship with Mattie. "Later."

Upon ending the call, curiosity got the best of Joey as he scrolled through his missed texts. Below a dozen unanswered messages were Mattie's. Tapping on her name, he read what she had to say.

*Mattie (9:48pm): I just saw your FB post and OMG! I know you're pissed at me but can we please move past it? I can't believe you never told me you're gay. I hope it's not because you thought I wouldn't be okay with it or something. That would break my heart. You know me better than that. Things got fucked up but I would never do anything to hurt you. I'll always stand by you, whether you're gay, straight, purple, or blue.*

*Mattie (9:56pm): I get that you're mad. I would be angry if what happened to you had happened to me. I hate that I had any part in it.*

*Mattie (10:09pm): I miss you. This is the first Christmas in four years that I haven't come over for dessert. It feels so weird to not talk to you. Does it feel weird to you?*

*Mattie (10:32pm): You might think that this is the end of our friendship, but I know it isn't. We're too important to each other to let it all go over this. I'm not minimizing how badly I fucked up at all. I'm painfully aware that my petty bullshit with Lilly caused all of this. I'm sorry. I really am.*

Joey sniffed and pressed a knuckle against the corner of his eye. He wasn't going to cry. There was no way he would allow even one tear to drip down his cheek. The whole night had been overwhelming. He'd finally come out and it was as if a huge weight had been lifted from his shoulders only to be replaced by the one he had tried to forget for the past three weeks. He didn't want to fight with Mattie. He wished she'd never done what she had, and he wished he had the ability to get over it.

Determining that he didn't want to read the rest of Mattie's texts,

Joey placed his phone on the nightstand and cuddled into the fetal position. He was going to enjoy the last few hours in his bed in peace.

## 32

Being back at Horizons after spending Christmas at home was dreadful. The fluorescent lights were more institutional, the walls more stark, the smell more antiseptic. The warmth of the holiday house had ruined him for rehab and made it even worse than it had been before, which was saying a lot.

Counting down the days until his release was a shitty way to pass time considering how depressing it was. Every minute was an hour locked in the prison of another name. Not only was the therapy exhausting, the loneliness was unbearable. Though he shared a room with a seventeen-year-old stoner named Adam, the company wasn't exactly comforting. Adam came from an affluent family in Chesterfield, and his stint in rehab was nothing more than a polite slap on the wrist from an exasperated mother. Adam was spoiled and had expected the place to be like the programs celebrities went to, complete with yoga and juicing. Horizons was much more bologna than beluga caviar, a fact that Adam made sure to mention at least ten times a day. Joey hadn't exactly grown up impoverished, but he found it slightly entertaining to play up his fondness for gas station nachos. Adam would respond by looking at Joey like he had admitted he ate garbage out of dumpsters, and Joey would double down by waxing poetic about some of the money-making schemes he'd participated in.

"You did what?" Adam uttered, sitting up in his bed to stare at Joey with disgust.

Grinning at his roommate's grimace, Joey replied, "It was pretty epic."

"Let me get this straight," he began, raising a finger as though Joey was going to interrupt him. "You stood in front of a free parking lot across from Busch and charged people to park there?"

Joey nodded. "Yup. It's not that complicated. We charged, like, twenty bucks a car and made fucking bank 'cause the garage across the street charged thirty."

"And they didn't question why some toddler-looking kids were collecting the money?" Adam inquired skeptically.

"No. They thought they were getting a deal. That's ten dollars off," Joey said, "They weren't going to jeopardize it by asking anything."

"You're a hoodlum," Adam asserted.

"And you're a sixty-year-old woman! Who the fuck says 'hoodlum?'"

"What should I call you? A thug?"

Cringing, Joey shook his head. "No. You're really not in touch with anything, are you?"

"Probably not," Adam admitted. "I'm not trying to be someone I'm not."

"Do you think I am?" Joey scoffed, eyeing the rich bitch down.

"Honestly, I don't know what to think of you."

"That feels like a compliment coming from you."

"Maybe it is," Adam relented, taking a swig from the water bottle he had beside his bed.

"Goddamn, this place is so weird. We probably would've never met if it weren't for marijuana."

"Wow, for the first time in my life you're gonna make me hate weed."

"Yeah, same."

"Maybe rehab works after all. Putting us together was a great way to make us swear off pot," Adam offered.

"I wouldn't go that far," Joey laughed.

"Yeah me either. I don't see what's so bad about the stuff. The counselors here keep saying it's the gateway drug, but the gateway to what? I'm not going to start shooting heroin. I mean, c'mon."

The gateway drug. Joey had heard it numerous times in regard to his father, but he had always doubted there was anything nefarious about weed, and his time in Horizons hadn't changed that opinion. What he had learned in rehab was that drugs weren't responsible for bad decisions. Sure, they messed with the brain and affected perception, but fault landed on a person more than what altered him. Drugs exacerbated what already lay under the surface. Joey wasn't worried about how he was made, and he didn't think drugs—even the strongest variety—could change that. The dumb things he did were on him. Maybe it would have been different if he were actually addicted to a substance. He abused drugs; they never abused him the way they had his dad.

Still, Joey recognized that he needed to make better choices, like not getting fucked up before school. Though the likelihood of expulsion was at an all-time high, Joey made a pact with himself to stay clean if he got back in—if not for any other reason than to simplify his life. He was sick of dealing with all the bullshit that came with getting in trouble. He didn't want to be anywhere but at home—not rehab, not juvie. If chilling on the weed was what it took to be left alone by therapists, administration, and just about everyone else, he was going to cool it. It was a matter of framing the intention as his own rather than one that was expected of him. His pervasive distaste for authority urged Joey to go in the opposite direction than the one he was meant to take, which only complicated his circumstances. It was cutting off his nose to spite his face, and he was done with it.

"Are you done with the conversation?" Adam asked. "It's unlike you to be quiet for two consecutive minutes. Did I say something that bothered you?"

"No, it's not that. I'm just thinking," Joey answered.

"And that takes a lot out of you?" his roommate teased, giving Joey a cheeky grin.

Stretching his arms over his head, Joey let out a lion yawn and settled deeper into his bed.

"Evidently." He was about to take a mid-morning nap when a knock on the door disrupted the plan.

"Joey, you have a visitor," the nurse announced, taking him by surprise.

"Really?"

It was Saturday. Bridget, Steve, and Paige typically came on Sunday. He couldn't imagine who would've come to see him, or who would've received approval from the facility. For a split second, Joey thought it could have been Mattie, but there was no way Horizons would've allowed a teenager who wasn't related to him to visit.

"Really," she confirmed. "Let's go."

Rolling out of bed, Joey slipped his Vans on and crouched to peek at the small mirror propped against the wall. "Who is it?"

"I'm not sure. I guess you'll have to see when we get there."

Joey's sneakers squeaked on the linoleum floor as he followed the nurse down the hallway toward the visitor's room. He stopped in his tracks as soon as he saw Mr. Seaver sitting at a table in the empty room. "What are you doing here?"

Seeing school personnel out of the context of school was weird. Instead of wearing his usual suit, Seaver was in jeans and a sweatshirt. His casual appearance was nearly as jarring as the fact that he was there to begin with.

"Hey Joey," the counselor said, standing up to shake Joey's hand. "Merry Christmas."

"Uh, Merry Christmas," Joey replied awkwardly, "You came all the way out here to tell me Merry Christmas?"

"That, and I wanted to talk to you."

"About?"

Seaver gestured to the chairs. "Take a seat."

Joey did as he was told. He never had anything against the older man, but Seaver wasn't exactly the first person he had expected to be on the visiting list.

"I've been worried about you," Mr. Seaver confessed.

"Why?" Joey questioned, bringing his index finger to his mouth so he could bite his nail.

"Honestly, why do you give a shit about me or what I do? You have tons of students to worry about."

"I do," Seaver agreed, tucking his hand into his back pocket. "But you've stood out for several reasons, the first of which is this." He placed a gold chip in front of Joey.

Glancing from the twenty-six inscribed on the chip to his counselor, Joey asked, "Is this yours?"

Mr. Seaver nodded and said, "Yup. Twenty-six years clean last month."

"Damn," Joey muttered in disbelief. He would have never taken Seaver for an addict. He thought the counselor had some fun back in his day, but Joey had figured he still kept his shit together. "I never realized ..."

"That I'm an addict? It's not something I talk about often. Believe me, I'm not ashamed anymore—it's the opposite, I'm proud of how far I've come—but in my line of work, it's not prudent to discuss such matters with impressionable minds."

"Wow, makes sense. Um, congratulations on twenty-six years, that's great."

"Difficult. It's difficult. I think about getting high every day, but do you know why I don't?"

"Why don't you?" Joey inquired, realizing he was about to get a tidbit of Seaver-brand inspiration.

"Because I don't want to mess up my life, man. It's as simple as that," Mr. Seaver said matter-of-factly. "One pill would be the start. It would unravel everything."

"Pills, huh?"

Seaver nodded. "Pills."

"Why are you telling me this?" Joey wondered, studying the counselor's slate-grey eyes.

"I know it's cliché, but you remind me a lot of myself at your age. I was charismatic, wild, uninhibited ... just like you are, but you have something that I never did."

"What's that?"

"Acceptance."

"Acceptance?"

"Acceptance," Mr. Seaver confirmed. "Which brings me to another thing we have in common."

Joey sat quietly in anticipation.

"I heard about your epic Facebook coming out post," Seaver began.

Laughing, Joey shook his head. "It was, like, ten words."

"Ten words other people are scared to say. Ten words I wasn't courageous enough to say until I was much older than you."

"Wait, you're gay?" Joey asked, confused. "You're married."

"To a man."

"Oh, shit. I probably shouldn't have assumed."

"Yeah. I spent a ton of time numbing myself so I could pretend I wasn't who I was, didn't want who I wanted. My parents were ..."—Mr. Seaver sighed and rubbed his forehead—"nothing like your mom and Steve. Let's just keep it at that. I've always rooted for you, even when you made it nearly impossible, because I wanted you to get out of this phase way faster than I did."

"I can stop whenever I want," Joey said, pausing when Mr. Seaver clicked his tongue with disapproval.

"You know that all addicts say that, correct?"

"I'm not an addict."

"They say that too," Mr. Seaver replied. "You're in the right place."

It wasn't worth arguing with the man who had come to support him in such an unexpected way.

"Maybe."

"You are," Seaver assured. "That's why I come bearing good news."

Raising his eyebrows, Joey waved the counselor on. "And?"

"I wrote the school board a letter on your behalf."

"Again?"

"Tell me about it," Seaver scoffed. "Deja Vu."

"No doubt."

"Anyway, I told them we failed you as an institution. We can't expect an addict to get clean by only providing the opportunity for punishment. You needed more intense counseling than I had the time to give you. We set you up to fail."

Joey was sure his face reflected the shock the rest of his body went through while listening to Mr. Seaver's statement.

"You look surprised," Seaver noted.

"I am."

"Well, they said they'd take my points into consideration when discussing your status at school. And eventually, maybe we can partner with a non-profit counseling organization to provide PHS students who struggle with similar issues more support," Seaver explained. "I'm not holding my breath for major program changes, but it's a start."

"It is," Joey agreed, floored by the passion his counselor had for reformation. Maybe they weren't as dissimilar as Joey had initially thought. After all, he had big ideas too. "Thank you for everything. I mean, even if it doesn't work out, I appreciate it."

"I hope this place helps you. Really take the time to learn what they're teaching. Maybe one day you can get one of these too." He took the chip and looked at it proudly before slipping it back into his pocket.

When Mr. Seaver stood up, Joey did as well. Without a word, Joey moved forward to give his counselor a hug. Perhaps they both needed it.

## 33

The new year didn't carry with it a new Joey. He was unconvinced anything could change him. Rehab and Mr. Seaver had given the challenge a valiant effort, and despite the impact both had on him, he wasn't going to magically become someone else to appease the masses or the handful of people who actually gave enough of a shit to be invested. It wasn't that Joey wanted to be a disappointment, it was more that he was positive he would be. Even early in his life, he'd vowed not to live for anyone but himself. Being loved by his mother never seemed to be contingent on a specific code of conduct, which had given him a freedom many kids weren't blessed to have. Sometimes Joey wondered if his mother's commitment had been an allowance to do whatever he wanted. If he thought that he could actually lose her, would he have ever taken the risks that he had?

The month at Horizons may not have altered Joey's future behavior the way most hoped it would, but it did reaffirm how important his family was to him. The last thing he wanted to do was be anywhere but at home.

Dropping his bag in the foyer, Joey climbed the stairs, excited to spend some alone time in the room that had felt like a prison thirty days earlier.

"Dinner's in an hour," Bridget called after him. "I'm making your favorite."

Joey's stomach growled in anticipation of his mother's biscuits and gravy. Though he had given Adam a lot of shit about his complaints regarding the food at rehab, Joey couldn't deny that his roommate had been right. His already thin frame felt slighter after his stay. He was ready to put some of Bridget's home cooking on his bones.

Aside from chilling with his family, he wanted to spend some quality time with his phone. Being without it had kept him worlds away from everything. As exhausting as he found high school to be, Joey missed the sociability and gossip the acquaintanceships provided. School wouldn't have been that bad if not for the rules he was expected to follow. If there were less of them and more art classes, Pacific High School would be a pretty cool place.

Joey dropped his phone on the bed and walked to the closet. Though social media was enticing, the reminder of his paints and pencils drew him in. Grabbing his pad and supply box from the top shelf, Joey laid them out on the floor in the center of his room. It was nice to have the capability to even look at his things. He had realized that creating was important to him prior to rehab, but the inability to focus on art while he was there solidified what an important place it had in his life. As much as he wanted to get lost in a new piece, he knew he should wait. Bridget would call him to the table, and he would get irritated by the interruption. She would probably rope him into a family game of Monopoly once they finished their meal, but after that was over with, Joey would enjoy some solitude by putting on music and starting a new sketch.

A light knock on the door was followed by Paige letting herself into his bedroom.

"Why knock if you're not going to wait for me to tell you that you can come in?" Joey wondered, standing up to give Paige a hug.

"I missed you," she said, snuggling her face into the nook of his neck.

He grinned and squeezed his sister tighter. "You saw me ten days ago."

"But now you're back for good."

"I hope so."

Paige pulled back to look Joey in the eyes. "What do you mean?"

"Who knows," he shrugged. "I mean, I don't want to be anywhere else, but I didn't expect to be in Jefferson City for a month either. Shit happens."

"Shit has a lot to do with our decisions," Paige reminded, twisting her hair into a messy topknot. "I figured you would come to that realization while you were in rehab."

"I did," he stated, sitting on his bed.

Paige stepped over the assorted art supplies that were splayed across the floor to join him.

"You're not a saint either," Joey pointed out. "You do the same drugs as me."

"Yeah, but I'm not dumb about it. I never get high before school, and I definitely wouldn't if I knew I would be tested every week."

"I had the process down," Joey stated.

"Until you didn't," Paige retorted, shaking her head. "You were gambling with your freedom, and you knew it. Then, after you dodged the bullet, you decided to smoke some crap you'd never tried before during first period."

"I'm not even going to try to argue that that wasn't dumb as hell. I know it was."

"So, Horizons was good for something," Paige smirked.

"A few things," Joey confirmed. "It made me really fucking grateful for Mom. Do you know how many of the people there had nightmare moms?"

"I'm guessing a lot of them."

"Most of them."

"Well, we're lucky," Paige said, pulling her phone out of the pocket of her sweatshirt.

Joey noticed the way the corners of his sister's lips turned up and how her eyes sparkled as she read a text. He knew that look even if he hadn't felt it himself. "Who's that?"

"Hmm?" Paige hummed as she rapidly typed her response.

"Don't tell me you're talking to—" he began but was interrupted by an emphatic "No" from Paige. "Good. Who is it then?"

"This guy in my Anatomy class," she replied vaguely.

"That's convenient."

Rolling her eyes, Paige refocused her attention on her phone screen.

Joey craned his neck to get a peek at her conversation and chuckled at the number of emojis in his sister's reply.

"Get the fuck outta here!" Paige cried, kicking Joey's shin.

"You're in my room."

"That isn't an invitation to read my texts," Paige tsked. "There's nothing interesting anyway."

"I saw an eggplant."

"You wish you saw an eggplant," she giggled. "Pervert." She shook her head as she went back to her messages while mocking Joey's statement, "I saw an eggplant."

"Whatever," Joey muttered, reaching for his phone. As usual, he had missed texts from Mattie.

*Mattie (6:03pm): I heard today was the day you got out of rehab. I'd love to see you and talk things out.*

*Mattie (6:04pm): Or just see you and not talk about any of this. Can we be done with it?*

*Mattie (6:10pm): Honestly, I'm happy you're home even if you plan to ignore me during our shifts.*

*Mattie (6:11pm): I miss you.*

He missed her too. He wasn't ready to admit it, but he did. There was something to be said for how persistent she'd been in trying to patch things up. Joey would have never fought for the relationship the way Mattie did, not because he didn't think it was worth it, but because he doubted anything was. It was weird not talking to her, not being told what was going on in her life, not getting shit for what he was doing in his. When he considered the situation and gave Mattie the benefit of the doubt, he saw a future for their friendship. It was easier to hold a grudge than to admit that maybe he'd overreacted and displaced the blame. He would never agree with Mattie being a narc, but it was a stretch to think that any of her actions were meant to hurt him.

*Joey (6:23pm): Sometimes I miss you too.*

The admission led to an instantaneous phone call that he promptly ignored. He was willing to open the door a crack but that was it. Knowing Mattie, she would attempt to take thousands of miles from the inch he'd given her. It was one of the things he used to love about her, a quality he could've learned from if he were open to it. He wasn't sure he was.

*Mattie (6:26pm): Pick up your phone then.*

*Joey (6:26pm): I'm not there yet.*

*Mattie (6:27pm): Yet means you think you could be one day. That's progress.*

*Joey (6:27pm): I don't know.*

*Mattie (6:28pm): Yes you do. If you didn't, you wouldn't have answered at all. I know you.*

His mom's exclamation that, "Dinner's ready!" had him dropping his phone like it was a hot potato that he didn't want to get stuck with. A prolonged connectivity hiatus suddenly didn't seem like a bad thing. He needed everything to settle down before he could think about taking anything else on.

"I've been looking forward to the 'welcome home' meal since you left," Paige confessed, shoving her phone into her pocket and jumping up from the bed.

"*You've* been looking forward to it?" he scoffed. "When I tell you that the food was fucking awful there, I'm not exaggerating. It was like the leftovers of what they give to people in actual prisons."

"How would you know what they serve in prisons?" Paige challenged. The scent of childhood celebrations wafted through the air as they walked downstairs to the kitchen.

"I watch TV," Joey replied. "There's at least ten shows about life on the inside."

"And you think they're real?" she asked skeptically.

"I watched a dude melt the ass end of a toothbrush down so he could shank another motherfucker on the yard," Joey answered. "They're real."

"Wow," Steve said, seemingly flabbergasted by the statement he must have overheard. "It sounds like you had a wild time at Horizons."

"He's talking about a prison show he watches," Paige clarified as she nudged Bridget out of the way in order to check on the gravy bubbling in a pot on the stovetop.

"But really there's not much of a difference," Joey informed them, smiling at Nicole as she approached him with her arms open. "How's it going?"

"I should be the one asking that," his step-sister stated. "We've missed you."

"Yeah, same," Joey assured. "I've missed you guys too."

"Especially his mama," Paige added.

The comment had Bridget beaming and shuffling across the floor in her pink fuzzy slippers to give Joey a hug.

In that moment, he doubted that any high could feel as good as finally being home.

# EPILOGUE

Things didn't work out the way his parents and Seaver had hoped they would. The School Board denied his re-admittance into Pacific High School. Mr. Seaver had big dreams on a small budget, and admitting Joey had needed rehab to begin with would have given the school culpability they weren't willing to take. Joey didn't blame the Board for following through with the expulsion he more than deserved, and he didn't fault the adults in his life for wishing he didn't deserve it.

"There are worse things than getting kicked out of school," Joey told Bridget as she dabbed her eyes with a wad of tissues she'd angrily balled up in her hand.

"Not right now," she warned. "Let me mourn this."

"I could be dead. Then you'd really be mourning," he said, earning an unimpressed glare from his mother.

"The death of your future feels like a good reason to cry, Joey."

"That's, like, crazy dramatic, Ma," Joey tsked, sitting down on the couch beside her. "I'm going to be fine. Pacific High School isn't the fast track to success, and you know it. Besides, there are other schools."

"There are, but you haven't been driven to look at any of them," she stated. "Does that change now that we've finally gotten the news? Because I'll sign you up for an online program tonight."

"I have to let the devastation of this loss pass before I get involved with another school," Joey explained, barely able to keep a straight face thanks to the smack his mother delivered to his arm.

"Quit it," she sighed. "Don't make fun of me while I'm depressed about the dumb shit you do."

"If you keep letting the dumb shit I do upset you, you're gonna be sad for the rest of your life." While Joey's statement was tinged with humor, he was serious. He didn't want that for his mother, but he couldn't pretend to be a person he wasn't.

Online courses remained an option, but Joey wasn't going to rush to enroll. As disappointing as it would be to Bridget, school wasn't his top priority—working at D'Antonio's so he could make enough money to get out of Pacific was. He had missed his family when he was away, but he couldn't stay in a place where his whole life was stagnant. He needed to be surrounded by the world in motion, not a town that moved only when it was pushed. The good thing about having family who cared about him—besides the obvious—was that they would find him wherever he went to find himself.

"It's my job to make sure you don't make stupid decisions that will mess up the rest of your life," Bridget said, tossing the saturated tissue aside to grab a dry one. "And I'm failing you."

"You have to stop looking at all of this like it's a bad thing. You didn't raise a robot who was programmed by society to be a clone of everyone else. That's pretty badass. You should be proud of yourself."

Bridget regarded Joey as though he were an alien sent from another planet to confuse the shit out of her, and Joey just smiled back. He had always been convinced that he knew who he was and understood why he made the decisions he did, had the beliefs he had. He shouldn't have doubted his conviction when things got difficult, but he did. There was no use in getting worked up just because there were twists, turns, and complications. It was all a part of the ride, and he'd never been scared to jump on.

"I don't think this is going to be the last thing I do that's going to piss you off," he added.

"Probably not," she relented, standing up and signaling for Joey to do the same, "and if we don't get to work you're going to piss Krysta off."

The car ride to work was lighter than the conversation they'd had moments prior, full of the teasing and laughter more common in their relationship.

"Have a good first night back and text me when you're done," Bridget said, pulling her car up to the front of the restaurant.

Joey waved behind him as he opened the door to D'Antonio's. It had been nearly two months since he'd worked a shift, and he was looking forward to focusing on something other than himself, even if it was slinging pizza.

"He returns!" Ernesto announced when Joey entered the kitchen.

Joey grinned, glad to see the cook's mischievous face after such a long time away. "What's up?" he greeted, slapping the hand that Ernie offered under the pass.

"You tell me. You're the one out there living an interesting life."

"That's one way to put it," Joey chuckled.

"Bridge calls it something different," Ernie teased, sprinkling parmesan on the pie he'd retrieved from the oven.

"I bet she does."

Joey tied an apron around his waist and clocked in, ready to get down to business. He was about to ask Krysta what section he had when he found himself face-to-face with Mattie.

"Matilda," he said as coolly as he could when calling Mattie by the playful name.

"Joseph," she replied, exhaling a giggle as tears welled in her eyes. "It's good to see you."

Joey nodded, tucking his hands into his pockets. It was good to see her too. It was easier to hold onto his anger when she wasn't standing in front of him, looking like the friend he'd loved for so many years.

"I'm so sorry," she promised. "So, so sorry. I never meant to hurt you."

It was the same thing Mattie had been texting him for two months, but the pain in her eyes made him feel it.

"Don't you get sick of apologizing?" Joey questioned, taking a deep breath. Forgiveness was harder than he'd expected.

"I do. Maybe you should accept it so I can stop," Mattie replied, putting her hands on her hips. "It's time, Joey."

"You know I don't like to be told what to do."

"And you know I don't like apologizing, yet ..."

"Yet you did shit to apologize for," Joey reminded, wondering why Mattie's hard-ass approach didn't bother him as much as it would have in the past.

"No doubt, and you give enough of a shit about me to accept it. Don't you?"

Joey hummed a noncommittal "hmm" and shrugged his shoulders. He knew the answer and so did she. Enough was enough.

"Don't you?" she prodded with a knowing smirk on her face. She tickled his side and repeated, "don't you?"

"I do," he admitted, laughing and shoving her tickle-fingers away. "We're good."

"Just like that?"

"Just like that," Joey confirmed.

Jumping up to give Joey a hug, Mattie squealed with excitement. "Finally."

"Emily's gonna be happy."

"How about you?" Mattie asked. "Are you going to be happy?"

"Always," Joey promised, knowing it was the truth.

"Not just letting me back in," she clarified. "You've been through a lot."

"And I'll go through more," he said easily. "I think that's how life is, you go through shit and get more resilient. I'm not worried."

"Have you ever been?"

He nodded. "Yeah, and you know what it did for me?"

Mattie shook her head.

"Nothing."

"And you can just control that? It's normal to worry," Mattie reminded. "Ordinary people worry."

"You know what I'm not?" he began, a smile spreading across his face.

"Ordinary?"

"Ordinary," Joey confirmed.

And he was incredibly good with that.

# THE RISE UP SERIES

Book Four
July 2019

www.ingramcontent.com/pod-product-compliance
Lightning Source LLC
Chambersburg PA
CBHW030319080526
44584CB00012B/632